Overcoming Panic, Anxiety, & Phobias is the perfect little handbook for the anxiety sufferer. It's basic, simple, and state of the art.

> Cyma Siegel, R.N.
> Editor-in-chief, Publisher
> *The National Panic/Anxiety Disorder Newsletter*

Most patients with anxiety disorders are treated by primary care physicians, not psychotherapists. At last here is an excellent book we can recommend to reinforce therapy and help patients help themselves.

> Maurice Martin, M.D.
> Clinical Instructor
> Harvard Medical School

Babior and Goldman's book, *Overcoming Panic, Anxiety, & Phobias,* explains plainly and in clear English how to understand and deal with these disorders. It encourages patients to look at their disorders in hopeful terms and gives them practical strategies. This is truly a remarkable self-help book.

> Joel L. Becker, Ph.D.
> Associate Clinical Professor
> Department of Psychology, UCLA
> Instructor, Department of Psychiatry
> UCLA Medical Center

This book is a great resource. It was comforting to find out I was not alone, and that there are practical solutions to rid myself of unnecessary fear. I plan to give copies to friends and coworkers suffering from similar problems. This book is a must first step to regaining control of your life.

> Dominick J.
> San Diego, California

My number one resource for symptom reduction; comprehensive yet succinct, an invaluable daily reference for long-term recovery from all anxiety disorders.

> Julie Britz, M.S.W., Psychotherapist
> Harvard Community Health Plan

Overcoming

PANIC
ANXIETY
&
PHOBIAS

New Strategies to Free Yourself from Worry and Fear

Shirley Babior, LCSW, MFCC
Carol Goldman, LICSW

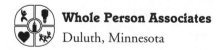

Whole Person Associates
Duluth, Minnesota

Whole Person Associates, Inc.
210 West Michigan
Duluth MN 55802-1908 218-727-0500

Overcoming Panic, Anxiety, & Phobias: New Strategies to Free Yourself from Worry and Fear

Printed in the United States of America

10 9 8 7 6 5 4

Editorial Director: Susan Gustafson
Art Director: Joy Morgan Dey

Library of Congress Cataloging in Publication Data
Babior, Shirley, 1938—
     Overcoming panic, anxiety, & phobias : new strategies to
free yourself from worry and fear / Shirley Babior, Carol
Goldman.
        176 p. 23 cm.
        Includes bibliographical references.
        ISBN 1-57025-072-3 (alk. paper)
        1. Panic disorders—Popular works.   2. Social phobia—
Popular works.   3. Anxiety—Popular works.   4. Self-help
techniques.
I. Goldman, Carol, 1950—   . II. Title.
RC535.B238   1995
616.85'22—dc20   95-42389
                                                                          CIP

To our families:
Bernie, Greg, and Jill
and
Bruce and Matthew

Acknowledgments

We are indebted to the pioneering work of Aaron Beck, David Barlow, Gillian Butler, David Clark, Diane Chambless, Michelle Craske, E.B. Foa, R.G. Heimberg, Debra Hope, Isaac Marks, L.G. Ost, and Claire Weekes.

Contents

Introduction

In the years since our book *Overcoming Panic Attacks* appeared, many of you—anxiety sufferers, their friends, loved ones, and therapists—have read our handbook and found it very helpful. We are delighted with your response.

It's now more than sixteen years since we began treating clients with panic attacks and other anxiety disorders as part of our clinical practices. We know that the techniques we teach help people recover from these debilitating conditions, but it's frustrating that many people are unaware of these techniques and therefore continue to suffer.

We wrote this latest book, *Overcoming Panic, Anxiety, & Phobias,* in response to the many letters we have received asking us to recommend strategies for coping with other types of anxiety problems as well as panic. In our private practices, we have noticed many similarities between the symptoms of people with a variety of anxiety disorders. We realized that the concepts in our book could be expanded and could therefore help many more people.

Fortunately, recent research on panic disorder as well as other anxiety problems has expanded the number, and to some degree the nature, of the treatments that work. Since experts know more about anxiety disorders of all kinds and since research has led to the development of new treatment strategies, the time seemed right for a new, expanded book. At the same time, we have tried again to keep the book short enough so you can it carry easily and consult it as often as needed in times of stress.

Whether you are working on overcoming a panic disorder or on another related anxiety problem, the ideas in this book will be useful as a key part of your recovery program. Even if your main goal is just to lower chronic stress and tension, you can learn important stress reduction tips from these pages. You may even be able to avert more severe forms of anxiety during future periods of intense stress.

In addition to reading this book and practicing the techniques described in it, we encourage you to seek help from medical and mental health professionals so that all factors contributing to your problem can be identified and treated. The suggestions for seeking professional help at the end of this book may prove helpful to you in selecting a therapist.

It remains very gratifying for us to watch or hear about a person's confidence growing as he or she recovers from panic or anxiety and begins to interact with the world more assertively and with more pleasure.

We wish you success on your path to recovery and are delighted that you are taking this book with you on your journey. We hope it helps. And we welcome your comments and suggestions.

Shirley Babior
Carol Goldman
1995

How to Cope
with Panic, Anxiety,
and Phobias

*Strategies to free yourself
from worry and fear*

Panic attacks are terrifying experiences that seem to strike suddenly and from nowhere! The sensations can be so extreme that you think your life is in danger, the feelings so painful that you dread, maybe more than anything else, having them happen again. You may find yourself on guard every waking moment, scanning situations for danger so you won't be caught by another surprise attack. The idea of being trapped by these paralyzing, painful fears is almost too much to handle. Are you dying? Or worse yet, are you crazy? Who can you confide in? What on earth can you do? Are you the only one who feels this way?

If you suffer from unexpected panic attacks, you know how devastating they are in your life, but you may not be aware that they impair the quality of life for millions of other sufferers—you are not alone. Fortunately, because this problem is now being addressed openly, embarrassment and shame need no longer keep people from seeking help.

As frightening as your symptoms and experiences are—and as unlikely as it may seem to you at the moment—you can get better. You can learn to manage these feelings. It will take work, and it will take courage on your part, but using the suggestions in this book, you, like thousands of others, can recover. At the end of each chapter, you will find stories of real people who made successful recoveries from anxiety problems as bad or even worse than yours.

Your symptoms may be different than those in these stories, but they can be just as distressing. Many people who suffer from stress and worry do not experience panic attacks. If this is true of you, instead of the acute, overpowering fear associated with panic, you may be chronically anxious, continually worrying about future events—including the possibility that you might be even more anxious later than you are now!

Many people struggle every day with panic and anxiety, but others face their terror only in specific situations. If you fear flying, public speaking, or small enclosed places, you may be able to function quite well when not confronted with those situations. If you have a specific phobia, however, you may find that it restricts your freedom and lowers your self-esteem.

As you read about a variety of anxiety problems, you may believe that your symptoms fit neatly into one category, or you may recognize in yourself elements of more than one anxiety problem. In the box on the following page, you will find some categories that are listed in the *Diagnostic and Statistical Manual* published by the American Psychiatric Association.

If you do not have one of these specific disorders but are experiencing a lot of stress and tension, read this book for general stress management. You will gain a variety of coping skills which can be used whenever pressure increases beyond what is comfortable and healthy for you.

> *NOTE: If you are experiencing severe depression or have an alcohol or other substance abuse problem, we urge you to seek professional help. Once these problems have been attended to, you will be ready to work with your therapist on your anxiety concerns. In addition, a thorough medical examination is essential to rule out an underlying physical disorder. When you have an examination and are given the okay, it will be time to learn to deal with your anxiety attacks in a new way.*

Anxiety Disorders

- **Panic disorder without agoraphobia:** Unexpected panic attacks accompanied by worry about the return of panic and persistent fears of life-threatening illnesses, losing control, or "going crazy." Common symptoms include dizziness, feelings of unreality, palpitations, shaking, sweating, and nausea.

- **Panic disorder with agoraphobia:** All of the above, plus anxiety when entering or avoidance of situations where a panic attack might occur and where escape is a problem or help would not be available. Common situations include crowds, bridges, tunnels, travel, waiting in lines, being alone.

- **Specific phobia:** Excessive fear attached to a specific object (animals, heights, blood, flying). The object or situation is avoided or provokes intense anxiety.

- **Generalized anxiety disorder:** Extreme, uncontrollable worry about multiple concerns, most commonly, financial, health, employment, and family safety. Physical symptoms may include fatigue, concentration problems, tension, and restlessness.

- **Social phobia:** Excessive fear of embarrassment in social, performance, or other evaluative situations. These situations are avoided or suffered with intense discomfort.

What is happening to me?

If you suffer from some form of anxiety, what is happening to you may seem overwhelming and confusing. Understanding the problem is the first step towards controlling it—so let's break these anxiety problems down into smaller parts to help you understand what is happening. Anxiety affects your physical sensations, your thoughts or images, and your actions. These elements are each important so we will describe them in some detail.

Your physical sensations

During a panic attack, physical sensations vary from person to person, but common symptoms are:

- heart palpitations
- chest pain or discomfort
- choking or smothering sensations
- dizziness
- stomach distress
- cold and tingling feelings in your hands or feet
- feelings of unreality or disorientation
- sweating
- faintness
- blurred vision
- trembling
- shortness of breath

These sensations can be very frightening, but remember, they are the body's normal response to perceived danger and are meant to protect you, not harm you. As you learn to understand this, you will soon find the initial stages of these sensations less frightening, and the symptoms will cease to become overwhelming.

In your case, if shortness of breath, for example, is your strongest and most troublesome symptom, this single sensation, associated with fear, can trigger panic. In an attempt to protect yourself, you might begin to monitor your breathing in certain situations, trying to detect the slightest change. Any perceived change in breathing, even when that change is due entirely to something simple, like exercise, can trigger fear which can lead to a panic attack. When the initial, mild signs of anxiety due to exertion or excitement no longer frighten you, you will be well on your way to recovery.

If anxiety usually strikes you in social situations, a physical symptom such as profuse sweating or a feeling that there is a lump in your throat or blushing or trembling hands may bother you most, and you may feel devastated when it occurs.

If your problem is generalized anxiety, you may be plagued by chronic muscle tension, jitteryness, a feeling of always being on edge, trouble concentrating, or feelings of fatigue.

Becoming aware of which physical symptoms you experience during mild, moderate, or severe levels of anxiety will allow you to observe that your anxiety is not always at its highest level. In order to become more aware of your own symptoms and begin to overcome your fear of what is happening in your body, turn to the "Anxiety and Panic Responses" worksheet on page 8, and fill out Part I by identifying a recent experience during which you felt anxious. Continue with Part II, Section a. by listing your physical sensations during that episode. You may want to photocopy this and the other worksheets in this book so you will have blank forms on which to keep track of your progress. Extra copies are printed in the back of the book.

You are going to make a complete record of this experience, so begin by recording the approximate date and time that the episode occurred. On the page preceding the worksheet, you'll read how other people responded to these questions. Their answers may help you recall your own sensations.

Complete Part I and Part II, Section a. before continuing your reading. You'll find that this book will be much more helpful to you if you take the time to reflect on your own experiences even though it may make you feel uncomfortable when you do so.

Your thoughts

Every anxiety disorder involves negative thoughts: beliefs that something worrisome will happen to you or to others. The nature of these beliefs varies depending on your anxiety problem. For instance, if you have a panic disorder, you may fear dying or losing control. If you have a social phobia, you may fear behaving with others in a way that humiliates you. If you suffer from a generalized anxiety disorder you may be convinced that a disaster will occur to you or to your family or friends. Life feels out of your control.

In these anxiety situations, the persistent belief that something dangerous will happen increases the uncomfortable physical sensations in your body and the anxious thoughts in your mind. In the face of increasing distress, you may attempt to deal with your fear in one of several ways. You may try to:

- avoid thinking about whatever you fear,
- distract yourself from it, or
- focus on your thoughts of impending danger in hopes of averting disaster.

Unfortunately, these attempts to evade the problem and ignore the fear are often unsuccessful. In Part II-b. of the "Anxiety and Panic Responses" worksheet, record the thoughts that you had during the episode that you described in Part I.

Your actions

In an attempt to prevent whatever you fear from occurring, you may avoid situations that seem risky. Once this avoidance takes over and becomes a pattern, you can end up feeling like you're living in a straitjacket, unable to do many of the things others can do. In addition, panicky and phobic feelings give rise to an instinct to flee the immediate situation. This can lead to a hasty departure! If you feel less anxious when you escape, you strengthen your impulse to flee the next time you are in a scary situation.

These responses can actually make your anxiety worse by strengthening your belief that what you fear is dangerous, is likely to happen, and that you are helpless to protect yourself. You will soon see that by practicing the techniques and strategies in this book you can begin to challenge your fears and overcome them.

In Part II-c. of the worksheet, record the actions you took as the result of your anxiety response.

Karen and Ben's Worksheet Responses

Karen's daughter was fifteen minutes late coming home from a date.

a. Karen felt tense, short of breath, and had a stomachache.

b. She thought her daughter would never come home and imagined that she was in a car accident.

c. She paced back and forth and wanted to call her daughter's friends.

Ben's boss said that he wanted to meet with him.

a. Ben felt like he had a tight band around his chest. He was sweating, and his neck and jaw were tense.

b. He thought about what he might have done that was wrong; he worried about not being perfect; he feared that he would be fired and end up divorced and homeless.

c. He snapped at his coworkers, couldn't concentrate, watched the clock, and made repeated trips to the bathroom while waiting for his meeting with the boss.

Michael had to attend a social gathering where he was expected to entertain several of his law firm's important clients.

a. Michael felt hot, sick to his stomach, and found it difficult to breathe.

b. He thought that he would probably embarrass himself and his firm by being unable to socialize with these people. He was afraid that he wouldn't be able to stay in the room and that he might have a full-blown panic attack.

c. He spent most of the day trying to think of excuses for not attending the gathering. When he got there, he tried to stay close to the door so he could leave quickly.

Anxiety and Panic Responses
Targets for Change

Part I: Anxiety producing episode

Date _____ Time_____

What brought on your feelings of anxiety or panic?

_____

_____

Circle your anxiety level:

   0   1   2   3   4   5   6   7   8   9   10
   none   mild   moderate   strong

Part II: Anxiety and panic responses

a. Physical sensations

   List the physical sensations you felt during your anxiety response, e.g., dizziness, shortness of breath, blushing, sweating, muscle tension. Circle the three that frighten you most.

   _____

   _____

   _____

b. Thoughts and images

   List the thoughts you had when anticipating or experiencing your anxiety response, e.g., "I'm having a heart attack," "I'm losing control," or "Something terrible will happen."

   _____

   _____

   _____

c. Behaviors and actions

   List the behaviors you exhibited or actions you took as a result of your anxiety response. _____

   _____

The high cost of anxiety

Anxiety has a very high cost. It can rob you of the ability to live freely and can strain your relationships. It's embarrassing to reveal your problems to others, but hiding them can distance you from your friends and family. Secrecy means you have to create excuses in order to avoid getting into situations that you fear. These excuses often make you feel guilty and make others feel resentful. If you do share your fears with others, your need for reassurance or help from loved ones can create conflict. Sometimes they just don't understand.

Anxiety limits you. You may turn down promotions because you fear increased travel responsibilities. You may avoid social situations even though you're lonely. You may perform below your capabilities in social, career, or test situations. Do you dread office meetings in spite of being prepared or suffer through activities that others enjoy like the theater, dining in restaurants, or taking vacations? Does your capacity for contentment easily shatter? Are your relationships burdened by endless worries? If the answer to any of these questions is yes, then anxiety is limiting your opportunities for growth and preventing you from living your life fully and enjoyably. And as anxiety intensifies and avoidance or anxious apprehension increases, the problem gets worse. Understandably, you feel frustrated and angry when your efforts to control the anxiety are unsuccessful.

Record on the worksheet below the costs of your anxiety.

The Costs of Anxiety

Anxiety has hurt my relationships with _____

_____

_____

Anxiety has limited my life by _____

_____

_____

Anxiety can be exhausting, discouraging, and very depressing. However, here is some very good news for you.

The benefits of recovery

You can overcome anxiety problems! You can be free of the pain. Your life can return to normal again or perhaps be even better than it was before! You can experience the benefits enjoyed by the people who share their personal stories of recovery in this book. They made comments such as: "The sense of freedom and control is almost euphoric." "Now I know that I was afraid of things I didn't need to be afraid of. I have learned to fly again, literally as well as figuratively." "I used to be afraid of so many things, but now I feel that I'm living again."

As you read these wonderful accounts of recovery, which are located at the end of each chapter, you may think as many do when in the throes of extreme anxiety, "I can never feel like those people. They could not have been as anxious as I am." We assure you that each of these people did at one time suffer from a very disabling anxiety—they are writing about their experiences from much further along on the road to recovery.

You can get there too! Take a few moments and imagine that your anxiety is manageable and under your control. On the worksheet below, list the benefits you will enjoy.

Life Without Severe Anxiety

When I am free of severe anxiety, I will feel_____

_____

_____

I will be free to do _____

_____

_____

The anxiety continuum

Think of anxiety on a continuum from very mild to very severe. In its milder state, anxiety can enhance your life. In key moments, it can make you sharper, more energized, and more effective. In cases of real danger, extreme anxiety can make the difference between your safety and disaster. Your anxiety is serving you well if it is in response to a real threat. Once you can tell the difference between useful anxiety, which leads to effective action in the face of a real threat, and excessive anxiety in the absence of real danger, you will be well along your road to recovery.

Let's begin by understanding the worry and panic cycles and their roles in maintaining your anxiety. When you understand them, you can begin to find ways of breaking the cycles.

- The worry cycle often begins with a concern that something you fear is going to happen. Events in your life may have taught you to be on guard and to strive for control. Most anxiety sufferers are consumed with worry about what might happen next, continually asking themselves, "what if . . . ?" This anxious apprehension may become worse as you begin to constantly monitor whatever concerns you. In fact, for some people, the anxiety caused by the anticipation of danger is much worse than the anxiety they actually feel in a feared situation.

- As you start to worry, you may also notice uncomfortable physical sensations. Research has shown that people who experience excessive worry may actually be biologically predisposed to easily develop the physical signs of anxiety. Sometimes the worry cycle starts with these physical sensations. Of course, these reactions will, in fact, increase your anxiety. You may feel tense and find it hard to concentrate. Your thoughts and physical sensations may interrupt your ability to focus at the task at hand.

- And finally, you feel extremely anxious. Until you find ways to break the cycle, you can go around and around: the thoughts or images, the physical sensations, and the anxious behaviors increasing each time. One worry may follow on the heels of another, and the worry cycle can take over your life.

What are some of the specific worries involved in your worry cycle?

My Worry Cycle

My thoughts or images are _____

_____

_____

_____

My physical sensations are _____

_____

_____

My actions are _____

_____

_____

In addition to excessive worry and anxiety, you may also experience panic attacks.

Panic attacks are time-limited episodes of extreme fear or discomfort accompanied by distressing body sensations and terrifying thoughts. A feeling that something devastating is going to happen and an overwhelming urge to escape are common. After you've had this very unpleasant experience, even the slightest physical sensation of anxiety can set off the worry cycle, stimulating your autonomic nervous system and priming you for another cycle of panic.

Picture the way your body reacts when you are in real danger—in a fire, for example. Your heart starts beating more rapidly, your stomach may tense, you sweat and shake. You have activated the "fight or flight response," which prepares you to battle or flee from danger. During panic attacks, these same reactions occur, but they are triggered even though there is no real danger—they are false alarms. We can't always discover why this process begins, but those who experience panic attacks often have a tendency to be very aware of body sensations and may also have inherited a susceptibility to these attacks.

Typically, panic attacks are likely to start after an illness, a pregnancy, a drug experience, relationship problems, loss of a loved one, moving, or a period of prolonged tension and stress. After this "false alarm" reaction occurs a few times, it may begin to be cued in specific situations. This happens because the site of a former panic attack becomes scary by association.

Let's explore this process in detail. If you had a recent panic attack in a supermarket and your dominant sensation was a racing heart, just thinking about going back to the supermarket can raise your anxiety level and cause your heart to race. It is not really the market you fear—it's the likelihood of your having a panic attack while you are there!

You feel vulnerable because of your past experience. However, it's crucial to understand that what you really have developed is a fear of your own sensations of panic. This fear has spread by association to the location itself. Some of the common sites associated with panic are crowded places such as stores, churches, theaters, subways, buses, and restaurants. Panic can occur almost anywhere you feel trapped or in danger—at the dentist, at work, in a social situation, waiting in a line, in a classroom, on bridges, in tunnels, in cars or airplanes, and sometimes right at home.

The intensity of your fear may vary from day to day, causing you to wonder about your sanity and creating fluctuations in your ability to face or avoid the situations you dread. Sometimes you can face these situations only with a trusted companion.

As the panic cycle begins to take over your life, you may also begin to become fearful of all kinds of sensations and activities you previously experienced as normal. Suddenly, the physical sensations associated with exercise, sex, or watching exciting movies may cause these activities to become frightening. As you begin to closely monitor your body for any signs of anxiety, this hypervigilance can itself trigger anxiety and panic during harmless activities.

More and more places and activities may begin to trigger attacks. To avoid them, you become increasingly vigilant and therefore prone to more attacks. Although you may feel powerless, you can break out of this vicious cycle that will otherwise increasingly take over your life.

First, take a look at your current situation. If you experience panic attacks, fill in your panic cycle on the worksheet below.

My Panic Cycle

My panic attacks are triggered by _____

_____

My physical sensations are _____

_____

_____

My thoughts and images are _____

_____

_____

My actions are _____

_____

Other activities and places that I now fear include _____

_____

The road to recovery

You have a greater capacity to control your anxiety than you may now believe.

We will share with you what we have learned from hundreds of anxiety sufferers about the techniques they have used to free themselves from their anxiety problems. In this book, we combine their insights with the latest clinical and research advances in the treatment of anxiety disorders.

How can you reverse the debilitating cycle of worry, anxiety, and fear? You have already begun the first step on the road to recovery by seeking to understand what is happening to you. The second step is to develop a new set of coping strategies that will enable you to analyze, as realistically as possible, the likelihood of immediate or future danger and the severity of any consequences. The final step is to challenge your assumptions about danger and begin to face panic and anxiety and any associated situations and feelings.

Fortunately, there are helpful ways to overcome anxiety problems and many concrete strategies to help you succeed. We will cover each of these topics, step by step, to prepare you to challenge and then conquer your problem.

This book is full of strategies and techniques for overcoming anxiety. You can personalize them by creating your own First Alert cards. On 3"x 5" file cards, record the statements and key words that are meaningful to you—the main ideas you want to remember. Read the cards when you are anxious or in a panic-related situation. Refer to them throughout your recovery for instant guidance and support. Read them when you are relaxed, and you'll realize how much progress you've made in conquering the problem.

Rating your feelings of anxiety, tension, and panic

Think of your feelings of anxiety on a scale from 0 to 10. Let 0 stand for totally relaxed and 10 for the very worst feeling of anxiety or panic you've ever experienced.

By rating your feelings in this way, you will begin to differen-
tiate between your levels of anxiety. We've included a form on the
next two pages to help you. Now, whenever you feel any anxiety,
you can assign it a number on this scale. Rating your own anxiety
level is very helpful so that you won't always anticipate the worst
possible attack. When you are aware that you feel low levels of
anxiety as well as high ones, you will have time to respond to mild
anxiety in ways that can calm you instead of alarm you.

For example, as you enter a shopping mall or social gathering
you may experience mild (level 3, for example) heart palpitations
or a slight feeling of shakiness. You may begin to take short,
shallow breaths, which will exaggerate your symptoms. However,
remembering that a less anxious response is possible, you will
have time to slow down and begin using some of the relaxation
methods covered in the next chapter. Relaxation methods, including slowing your breathing, can dramatically reduce the
physical symptoms of anxiety and help avert spiralling anxiety
and full-blown panic.

Anxiety Rating Scale

Many people can't discriminate between different levels of anxiety or panic. They feel either calm or anxious. To help you become aware of your own intermediate levels of anxiety, complete this worksheet form, being as specific as you can.

As you experiment with the coping strategies you will be learning, refer to this worksheet in order to discover what strategies work best for you at different levels of anxiety.

Level 10: extreme anxiety

When my anxiety is at level 10, my thoughts are _____

_____

_____

My bodily sensations are _____

_____

_____

My behaviors include _____

_____

Level 8: on the verge of extreme anxiety

When my anxiety is at level 8, my thoughts are _____

_____

_____

My bodily sensations are _____

_____

_____

My behaviors include _____

_____

Level 6: severe anxiety

When my anxiety is at level 6, my thoughts are _____

_____

_____

My bodily sensations are _____

_____

_____

My behaviors include _____

_____

Level 4: moderate anxiety

When my anxiety is at level 4, my thoughts are _____

_____

_____

My bodily sensations are _____

_____

_____

My behaviors include _____

_____

Level 2: mild anxiety

When my anxiety is at level 2, my thoughts are _____

_____

_____

My bodily sensations are _____

_____

_____

My behaviors include _____

_____

Before you begin learning techniques for overcoming anxiety, take a few minutes and on the worksheet on the next page, list your goals for recovery.

As you continue reading this book and learning new strategies, return to this worksheet, fill in the action steps needed to reach your goals, and begin practicing them.

Matt's Responses to the "Goals" Worksheet

Matt found that his body's response to activities such as biking was making him anxious and causing him to avoid physical exertion. Matt wrote:

Goal 1: My goal is to reduce my feelings of panic and my fear of having a heart attack while riding my bike.

To accomplish this I will:

1. Practice breathing exercises twice daily.

2. Complete practice sheets in this book.

3. Practice sensory exercises twice daily.

4. Ride my bike regularly.

Goal 2: To be able to ride in next summer's bike race without feelings of panic before or during the race.

To accomplish this I will:

1. Learn how to handle the first symptoms of anxiety without allowing them to become a full-blown attack.

2. Challenge myself with increasingly difficult bike rides.

3. Send in my registration without procrastinating.

4. Learn how to handle any setbacks that I might have without becoming discouraged.

5. Ride in the race for the pleasure and confidence it will give me to complete it without anxiety.

My Goals

List two to four goals you'd like to achieve in the next one to three months. Fill in the action strategies as you learn new coping skills.

Goal 1 _____

Action strategies to achieve my goal:

     a. _____

     b. _____

     c. _____

     d. _____

Goal 2 _____

Action strategies to achieve my goal:

     a. _____

     b. _____

     c. _____

     d. _____

Goal 3 _____

Action strategies to achieve my goal:

     a. _____

     b. _____

     c. _____

     d. _____

Goal 4 _____

Action strategies to achieve my goal:

     a. _____

     b. _____

     c. _____

     d. _____

~ ~ ~

The people whose stories are printed below had severe and long-standing problems with anxiety and panic. If they could recover, you can too!

Terri's story

I've had anxiety situations most of my life. As a child I was afraid to sleep over at a friend's house, afraid of summer camp, afraid of leaving my parents. The first semester away at college it all hit me. After final exams, I was going home to be with my family and I had an unbelievable panic attack on the airplane.

After college I became practically housebound. I missed work for three months. I started avoiding more and more situations until I just couldn't do anything anymore. I was too afraid to tell anyone about my fears, because I thought there was something wrong with me. I was anxious anywhere, everywhere, anytime.

I tried to explain what was happening to my boyfriend. I told him, "It feels like I'm on a little bridge on the top of a cliff and people are saying, 'Just walk off. Don't worry. Everything will be okay.' " I would think in my head, "How can they tell me that everything is going to be okay when I'm going to walk off this cliff and die?"

I went to a counselor, but at first, I couldn't even get to the floor where the office was because I couldn't take the elevator. I remember thinking, "Well, it can't be any worse than I'm feeling right now." Even being in the counselor's office scared me, that's how bad it was.

Gradually, I began to relax, making progress in one situation after another. The dizziness I feared went away with the breathing exercises I learned. Also, I had to expect not to feel confident about a situation that had been scary before. I just had to believe that I would be okay.

Worrying about things beforehand was my biggest problem. Situations were never, ever as bad as I had imagined them to be. To reduce my anxiety, I tried to figure out what the worst realistic outcome might be, and then decide what I could do about it. Then I realized that I could handle whatever might happen.

People need to know that even though things will go up and down, meaning better and worse, you'll never go as far back as you were before you started working on the anxiety attacks. I wanted to write my insights down because otherwise they just get forgotten.

I realized that a lot of the panic had to do with being a perfectionist. I was trying to be very fast-paced, trying to do too many things at once, accommodating everyone else in my life and never saying no. When I began to read books about panic attacks, I kept thinking, "Hey, this is me! This is exactly what I'm feeling!" I had such bizarre feelings and then, when I read about them, I felt, "Hey, I'm not nuts after all. They're not going to lock me up because I tell them about this." It was a huge relief.

While you are reading this book and my story, remember, you don't have to trust completely. Just leave open the option that there's a chance you'll get out of this. You don't have to feel like there is absolutely no hope. You can believe that since other people got out, you can too. I know you can because I did.

Margaret's story

I awoke one night out of a sound sleep with a racing, irregular heartbeat, difficulty breathing, and an incredible feeling of terror. I was twenty-seven then, and it was my first panic attack. I was petrified. My husband was out of town on a business trip, and I thought I was dying! When the attack finally passed, I went back to sleep and didn't think too much about it because it didn't happen again.

About a year later, I began having headaches and dizzy spells every day. I spent a week in the hospital having tests, and all the doctors and tests said I was "fine." However, little by little, more symptoms of panic attacks began to occur.

My husband and I loved to go out to dinner; this was about the only time we got to see each other, but then I began having problems in restaurants. I'd get severe headaches, feel faint and short of breath, and I even got nauseated. Basically, I started getting terrified. As a result, we stopped going to restaurants. Next, it progressed to me staying away from church, shopping, and friends' homes. The most frightening thing to me was that I was even beginning to have panic attacks at home. Nowhere was I safe.

Meanwhile, my children were getting older and more involved with sports and other after-school activities. My husband would have to take time off from work to drive them to these activities, or I would have to depend on my very friendly neighbors. I really hated this dependency on other people and the fact that all these people had such control over my life. My husband had to take the kids to dentists, doctors, haircuts, etc. Our entire Saturdays were spent doing errands that I could have done during the week if I could have driven. And I was always being told by my family and friends that I *should* be driving . . . and why wasn't I?

I really wanted to drive, but I was afraid even to be a passenger in a car. I was really caught in a dilemma. I wanted the freedom and control of being able to drive, but I was afraid that if I did learn to drive, I'd never see my husband. It seemed that our Saturday errands were the only times we had to be together.

What really irritated me was that I was having difficulty handling stress at this time in my life, although for many years, I had handled lots of serious responsibilities and managed them well. Now my life was falling apart.

I went to my internist, and he suggested that I see a psychotherapist. I saw both my physician and the therapist for two years and was on medication, but progress was slow. Finally, in desperation, I turned to another medical doctor and another psychotherapist.

With the new doctor I went through all the physical exams again to rule out any heart or neurological problems. Everything was okay physically, but he suggested that I join an agoraphobic therapy group. That was the first time the word *agoraphobia* was used to describe my problem. I was a little skeptical about group therapy because I'm very shy and not a joiner. But to my surprise,

I found that I was actually participating in the group and feeling good about it. The first and most important thing I learned was that I couldn't die from a panic attack. So, every day the fear of dying was greatly lessened. With that out of the way, I was able to concentrate on how I was going to handle and maybe beat this problem.

One big step on this road to recovery was getting my driver's license. Instead of thinking about how scared I was, I took it a step at a time, got my learner's permit, tried to practice every day, took some lessons, and finally got my license in September on the first day of school, just in time to pick up my daughter. The look on her face when she saw me there to pick her up was my reward for all the anxiety attacks I had while learning to drive.

I've had my license for just a short time now, and I can't believe the difference in my life. The sense of freedom and control is almost euphoric. To be able to drive myself around is great. I finally feel like a grown-up again. Not only that, my husband is spending more time with us as a family, and we are making more time for the two of us.

Excerpted with permission from the *Greater Boston Phobia Society Newsletter.*

Betsy's story

My panic attacks started two-and-a-half years ago. I was attending college, and I began to have what I thought were colds. Later, it turned out that they were actually panic attacks. I broke out in a sweat for some unknown reason, and my heart raced. Also, although I didn't realize it, I hyperventilated. That made my panic worse, so I would call up my husband at work and he'd say, "Now breathe, sit down, calm down." But, as soon as I hung up, I hyperventilated again. In a short time, I thought I had a real physical disorder.

Nothing really helped. I just got worse. Eventually, if a plane flew over while I was driving, I got scared. I would just grab the wheel and shake. Eventually, I didn't leave my house. I avoided anything that took me out into the world by myself—anything I had to do alone, anything that required driving. I didn't want to leave my little cocoon because that's where I felt safe—but even that didn't even last for long. Soon I began to have problems with digestion. Then my appetite just disappeared. I couldn't seem to process food. Also, I had a lot of numbness in my arm, which worried me a great deal, and many days I felt dizzy. I decided the problem must be physical, so I began to go to doctors, but all the medical examinations came back normal.

Then I started reading books on panic attacks and learned more about the symptoms I was having, I began to get a little better, and my husband became more willing to go along with whatever I needed.

I began to see a counselor, and that was when I learned I had a need for approval. I had to be a good girl! In the process of going to therapy and trying to follow the practical advice I got, I challenged myself enough so that I began to see a little progress. Even though I thought I would never get better, I still kept trying to take it a step further each time. At first, I wanted to come back to my therapy session and tell my counselor that I had done better, but eventually, I just did it for myself.

As I began to make progress, there was one thing I was still afraid of. I thought I couldn't cope with working and having other people dependent on me.

Luckily for me, I just got thrown into work. My husband's office needed a receptionist. I had the ability to do what they needed, and we needed the money, so I said yes without thinking. When I started working, I realized there was nothing to panic over, and so within a week, I had the routine down and was doing fine. I also made some wonderful friends and did a good job.

Now, as I drive to work, I think of the days when I drove the freeway, gripping the wheel in a state of panic for fear I would pass out, seeing spots in front of my eyes, which were caused by my forced breathing. Every once in a while, I still discover myself holding on to the wheel with a vise grip, so I try to pry my fingers loose. I quickly remind myself that I'm okay, and I begin to relax. Now the freeway is like an old friend. It is my road home.

My advice to anyone having symptoms like the ones I used to have is to keep trying and never give up, because it's only by trying again and again that you get through this kind of ordeal. Just one step further each time, and eventually you'll make the trip to recovery!

Andrea's story

I began to realize that I had a big problem when I started to withdraw from people and feel funny when I left my house. For several years before that happened, I went to social functions, and when I got there, I felt the need to be the life of the party. Some people really enjoyed that, although other people, I thought, did not enjoy it at all. But after awhile, I thought that it was necessary to perform whenever I went out. I had to do impressions, tell jokes, and give one-liners.

But eventually, I consciously stopped performing and withdrew. I stopped going to parties because many times I felt out of place—like I didn't want to be there. I didn't want to dress up. I didn't want to be a part of the scene. Many times, I didn't want people to see me sick or anxious.

When I forced myself to drive to visit my sister in Los Angeles, I had to stop the car three or four times to go to the bathroom because I was scared. I had a lot of trouble with hyperventilation. One year, my husband and I went to San Francisco during the Christmas holidays. It was supposed to be a romantic trip for us. But while we were there, the muscles in my forearms, legs, hands, mouth, and feet became limp, and I could not talk. I had motor problems as well. My husband had to call emergency, and the paramedics came out. They took me to the hospital, checked me out, and then released me because I had no real physical problem. I slept for two days in the hotel room, and I never did see San Francisco. The result of that experience was that I completely lost confidence in traveling and tried to get out of it as much as possible.

Although I could manage the freeways if I was driving, when someone else was driving, there were times that I had severe panic attacks, anxiety, and cold sweats. I would actually have to get out of the car. Ironically, this did not occur in airplanes, maybe because I don't know how to drive airplanes!

I am a lot more easy going now. I have a couple of dogs. I don't worry about things around the house, about traveling, or about my job. I used to worry that I would go crazy and end up as a street person, I was afraid that I could not hold down a job because I was sick all the time, was exhausted from insomnia, and was unable to go on business trips. I feared that I would get divorced, lose my home, and become a ward of the state. I thought a lot about those things.

But I have a lot less anxiety now, and I am more relaxed. I am able to travel whenever I choose to. When I feel tense, I practice with the relaxation tapes I have made, and I am able to examine my anxious assumptions and understand them for what they are. The world is a much better place for me. I think what helped me most is the awareness that I do not have to be perfect, prim, or proper. I can just be me. That is just what I have been doing.

Practicing New
Ways to Relax

Techniques for reducing the
physical symptoms of anxiety

Whatever anxiety problem you experience, it probably causes
you to hold a lot of physical tension in your body. You may feel
wound up or pressured. Your muscles may feel tight and sore. This
high level of discomfort can cause you to become more vulnerable
in stressful situations.

For this reason, we are including descriptions of simple techniques you can use to help reduce this general level of tension. Try
all of them to see which works best for you. When you find one that
works particularly well for you, write it on a First Alert card.

If you experience anxiety rather than relaxation while doing
these exercises, we encourage you to stick with them. Experiencing
low level anxiety will give you an opportunity to feel these physical
sensations and help you learn to interpret them as harmless.
Throughout the program in this book, you will be learning that
false danger alarms are opportunities to practice what you're
learning. For example, you can learn to think about what is really
happening at the moment, noting whether the tragedy you expect
does or does not occur.

Breathing

Many of the symptoms you experience may be related to the way
you are breathing. Feeling slightly nervous, you begin to breathe

shallowly, faster than usual, in short, choppy breaths or in forced breaths, all of which tend to increase the severity of anxiety symptoms. Hyperventilation, or overbreathing can be responsible for many of the physical sensations you fear: light-headedness, dizziness, blurred vision, heart pounding, feelings of unreality, and fatigue. For some people, breath retraining can dramatically reduce the level of anxiety or the number of panic attacks; for everyone it can be a powerful way to calm the body.

It's extremely helpful to practice slow, gentle breathing before and during a stressful situation. To be sure that you are breathing this way, inhale slowly and gently in through your nose, hold it for a second, and then slowly breathe out through your mouth, pursing your lips as if you are sipping through a straw. Try this technique now. Inhale to the count of six, pause, and exhale to the count of six. Don't give up too quickly. Your body needs time to respond to this unfamiliar, but normal, breathing pace. Continue taking slow breaths for a few minutes.

To check your breathing, put your hand on your stomach. If you are breathing slowly and from your diaphragm, you should be able to see your hand gently rise and fall as you inhale and exhale. If you continue breathing in this slow, calming way, often you will notice that your symptoms will be less severe and your level of anxiety will lower dramatically.

Another effective exercise combines slow breathing techniques with imagery. Imagine that you are lying on a beach, feeling the warm sun shining from above and the warm sand beneath you. Center your breathing in your diaphragm, repeating "warm" when you breath in and "release" when you breath out. As you do this, switch off your muscles, letting the tension go. The images of sun and sand work well in this exercise, but any images that you find relaxing will work. If you don't live near a sea coast, your most relaxing image may be lying on a picnic blanket on the lawn in the warm sun. Use whatever image is meaningful to release your tension.

Practice slow, gentle breathing for a few minutes two or three times each day. Continue this during calm intervals for a few weeks. Using the "Tension/Relaxation Rating" worksheet on the next page, rate your level of tension before and after you practice. This will provide you with feedback about your results. After practicing during uneventful times, begin to use slow, gentle breathing as a coping strategy during anxiety-producing situations.

Progressive muscle relaxation

Other exercises can also be effective to help you learn to relax when you experience a great deal of tension in your body. Even when you have nothing to fear, it's very likely that you are holding your muscles tightly, as if you had to prepare for a disaster. It's possible that you've never really learned to relax. If that is the case, learning to relax can help you deal with anxiety and panic attacks. Your body will be less stressed and you can practice physically letting go of tension when you begin to feel low levels of anxiety. Before and after each relaxation session, fill out the worksheet on the following page, recording your level of tension and describing the event, your thoughts, and your physical sensations.

One exercise that targets muscle tension and strain is called progressive muscle relaxation. Pick a time to practice when you are not rushed and will not be interrupted. In a quiet room, make yourself comfortable in a chair or lying down, and then begin to tighten and relax specific muscles in your body. First, slowly tense a specific muscle as much as you can, stopping short of causing cramping or pain, and then notice the feeling in the tight muscles. Next, release the tension and enjoy the pleasant feeling of relaxation. As you continue, study the contrast between the tension and the relaxation in each area of your body. While you are practicing, try to hold the muscles tense for at least five seconds, then relax for at least thirty seconds. Some parts of your body—your back, for example, which has many more muscles than other parts—may require more time. If you still feel tension in certain muscle groups after you finish tensing and relaxing them, you may choose to repeat the exercise before moving on.

Tension/Relaxation Rating

Rate your feelings before and after the relaxation exercise from 0 (most relaxed) to 10 (most tense).

Date	Before the exercise	After the exercise	List the events, thoughts, and physical sensations that had contributed to your feelings of stress.

Here are more exercises to try:

1. Wrinkle your forehead, trying to bring your eyebrows up to your scalp, noticing the tension at the bridge of your nose and over each eyebrow. Now release the tension and feel it slowly ease away.

2. Wrinkle your nose, and notice the tension at the bridge of your nose and nostrils. Pay special attention to the areas that are particularly tense. Now relax and notice how the muscles feel.

3. Close your eyes tightly. Now relax your eyes as you release the tension and notice the difference in how you feel.

4. Smile as widely as you can. Your lips and cheeks should feel tense. Now relax the muscles in your cheeks, and notice how they feel. Focus on the sensation of relaxation and what that is like for you.

5. Clench your teeth as hard as you can without causing pain. Push your tongue up against the roof of your mouth. Now relax your jaw and tongue, and think about enjoying the sensation of letting go.

6. Tighten your neck and shoulders, bringing your shoulders up towards your ears. Pay special attention to the areas where you feel tense, especially the back and sides of your neck. Now let go as much as you possibly can, letting your shoulders droop. Then let go a little more.

7. Make a fist in front of you, holding your arm out straight, and make your entire arm as rigid as you can. Notice how tense it is. Now relax and lower your arm, allowing your hand to fall naturally at your side. Again, notice how different it feels.

8. Raise your leg. Turn your toes up and back and make the whole leg rigid. Now slowly relax and lower your leg. Again, notice how it feels.

9. Bring your fists up high on your chest, pull them back and clench them as hard as you can. Notice how your shoulders and back feel. Now slowly open your hands and let your arms fall, noticing the difference.

10. While sitting down, tighten all the muscles below your waist as hard as you can. You should feel yourself rise off the chair a little. Notice where the tension is, especially the tops and bottoms of your thighs. Now, gently relax all of your leg muscles and notice the difference.

11. Now scan your entire body with your mind, retracing your path through all the muscle groups and concentrating on the feelings of relaxation in each set of muscles. If you notice any remaining tension, repeat the tension-relaxation exercise in that part of your body before continuing on to the next group of muscles. Notice that when you turn your attention to each set of muscles, they may relax even more. Savor these sensations of relaxation for as long as you like before ending the practice—the longer you linger, the more relaxed you may become.

Make a mental note to allow this relaxation to stay with you after you proceed to your next activity—no need to clench your muscles when you get up out of the chair—keep as many of your muscles loose and relaxed for as long as possible. Repeat this sequence of exercises as often as you can for one month—twice a day is optimal. You will notice that after a while it takes you less time and effort to produce deep relaxation. You may feel fully relaxed halfway through the exercises.

When this happens, you can abbreviate the exercises but get the same benefit by selecting the four muscle groups which give you the strongest relaxation response. Relax them in sequence, then finish with a body scan (see exercise 11 above).

After practicing for a while, you will be ready to use the exercises in real life situations. One way to do this in public is to practice relaxation by recall. Start by using your slow, gentle breathing. Then scan your body with your mind, focusing on each muscle. You will notice the feelings of relaxation begin when you think about a muscle group. Without actually doing the muscle exercises, the relaxation will happen automatically.

In situations where you feel anxious, you can use this technique to reduce muscle tension or to check your body for areas that may be tense. If you notice that frequently your neck, shoulders, or stomach muscles are tense, scan those areas to check for tension. Tense and relax the muscles in those areas or focus on the muscle and remember how relaxation feels.

Scan your body during activities such as driving, walking, or attending a meeting. Try to relax all the muscles which are not essential for a particular activity. For instance, while sitting on a plane, you can relax your face, neck, shoulders, legs, and feet while you keep tension in one arm to hold a book. Protecting yourself from unnecessary muscle tension will enable you to arrive at your destination refreshed, instead of drained. At the computer or while reading, if you relax your face, neck, shoulders, chest, and back, you may be able to work much longer without feeling stiff and fatigued.

Relaxation cues

Think of a cue word that is calming to you, such as calm, relax, or peace. Become aware of the tension in your body, experience it, and notice under what conditions it appears. Take some slow, gentle breaths. Say your calming cue word to yourself each time you slowly exhale. Release body tension with each exhalation. Concentrate on the physical sensations of relaxation, allowing yourself to become calmer and more in control. Use this quick and powerful relaxation technique whenever you feel anxious.

Mindful meditation

The goal with all of these exercises is to produce a feeling of physical well-being. Another way to achieve this is to practice mindful meditation. Sit comfortably, relaxing your body into a chair. Focus on your breathing, and when thoughts arise, without judging them, focus again on breathing. We have provided a script for you to read and to use for practice until you become used to this way of being comfortable with your thoughts and with your breathing. Practice 10 to 20 minutes daily, then begin to pause and take a few minutes for a mini-meditation during anxious moments throughout the day. In time, observe any changes in your awareness of fear. You may discover that you are more able to stay in the moment and are more comfortable and less frightened by your physical sensations and thoughts.

Taped relaxation scripts

Taped scripts are another device to use for relaxation. Instead of reading or trying to remember a sequence of steps, a familiar voice reminds you how to relax. On the next pages, you will find four short scripts that you or a friend can record. They should be read slowly and quietly. Pause briefly at the ellipses and for a longer period at the end of each paragraph. When you need to relax, play the tape. Sometimes it is helpful just to listen to the tape, even if you are not in a place where you can do the exercises.

If you find it more convenient, you can purchase a prerecorded tape that contains scripts adapted from this book and our book for therapists, accompanied by relaxing music. In the back of this book you will find information about ordering the tape.

Although you may feel anxious in your car, do not listen to relaxation audiotapes while driving, the risk of becoming drowsy is too great.

As you become increasingly familiar with these scripts and with the process and feelings of relaxation, you will find that you can quickly and easily relax by running through the script in your mind. You won't always have to have a tape recorder available.

Before you listen to a tape, make yourself comfortable. Close your eyes if appropriate. Focusing on the instructions will allow you to replace your inaccurate, scary thoughts with accurate, coping affirmations.

Script 1: Relaxation and imagery

Stretch your legs as far as you can, turn your toes back, and tighten all the muscles in your feet as tightly as you can. Hold it . . . tighten all the muscles in your calves and thighs. Make each leg rigid and hold it . . . hold it . . . now let your legs go completely limp and feel the relaxation in every part of your leg, in your toes, in your feet, and in your thighs. It's a wonderful feeling.

Now, stretch out your hands and make a fist. Make it tight, tighter, tighter . . . and hold it. Now make your arms rigid, and feel the muscles in your forearm and biceps. Hold it . . . hold it . . . good. Now relax, all the way. Let your arms hang limp, and notice how loose they feel, how relaxed.

Now arch your back, and tighten every muscle you can find in your back and neck. Make a face, as tight as you can, and hold it, hold everything . . . keep holding . . . keep holding . . . Now I am going to count backwards from 10, and as I do, I want you to think of a scene that makes you feel very calm, very relaxed, and while I am counting and you are visualizing that scene, I want you to slowly relax all those tense muscles. I am counting down now, 10, 9, 8, 7, 6, 5, 4, 3, 2, 1. Good. Now you are more relaxed, feeling less tension in your body, and you can feel the wellness spreading inside you . . . and on your face . . . and in your legs and shoulders. Good. Now just enjoy that peaceful feeling of relaxation. Soon you will open your eyes if they are closed. Good. All right, open your eyes. You feel very well and very relaxed.

Script 2: Breathing for relaxation

I may be frightened now. I may feel like running away. But stop! Listen! Everything will be fine. What I feel now will go away with time. This will pass. Nothing terrible will happen. I ask myself, "What is actually happening at this moment?" I notice the sensations in my body. I notice any scary thoughts. They cannot harm me. I am safe because my body will take care of itself. I am learning that although these sensations and thoughts are uncomfortable, they do not mean anything worse will happen.

I take a gentle, slow breath, inhaling slowly and evenly. I hold it . . . and exhale, slowly, slowly . . . my body can do this. I try it again—inhaling, slowly . . . holding it . . . exhaling, very slowly. While I exhale, I let myself slump, just letting all my muscles relax, like I am a rag doll . . . good. I let my shoulders hang down.

I know how much my scary thoughts, worry, and physical sensations have controlled my life. It is unfair that they should have that much control over me. I can complete what I set out to do because this fear will pass. It will pass.

I take another slow, gentle breath . . . hold it . . . and let it go, very slowly . . . I let my muscles go as I exhale, slowly. I will not worry if I become more aware of my fear . . . I will think about what is happening right this very minute. Where am I? What am I doing? What is actually going on at this very moment?

I am doing something very hard. I am choosing to feel these physical sensations now so that I can feel better tomorrow. I am being very brave, in a new way . . . these feelings will not harm me. I am safe.

I will try another slow, gentle breath through my nose. I inhale . . . hold it . . . and exhale, very slowly, letting my muscles go while I exhale. Good. I won't let these scary thoughts and feelings run my life. I will decide. I will choose to continue with what I am doing right now. I may feel more discomfort now, but on the other side of that discomfort is greater self-confidence and a better life. I am safe and I will feel better. The more I practice dealing with these scary feelings, the better I will become at coping with them.

Script 3: Cue words and imagery

While you are doing this exercise, you might want to put some pleasurable, soothing music on in the background and close your eyes if you feel comfortable doing so. Or, if you prefer, keep your eyes open. That's fine too. Make yourself as comfortable as possible.

Take a slow, gentle breath and say to yourself, "Calm and relax. Just relax." Relax more and more. Feel the relaxation in your forehead. Your forehead muscles are becoming loose, limp, and heavy. Just feel your eyelids relaxing. Allow your cheek and jaw muscles to relax more and more. Feel the relaxation in your neck and your shoulders and allow all the tension to leave your arms and your fingertips. Take another slow, gentle breath and as you exhale, say to yourself, "Calm and relaxed."

Take in another slow, gentle breath. Exhale and feel even more of the tension leaving your body. Continue your slow, gentle breathing. Each time you inhale, relax further and further. Each time you exhale, let a little more of the tension leave your body. Let the tension go wherever it wants to go. Just imagine your muscles relaxing more and more. Continue to breathe slowly and gently. Think about the journey you are going to be taking on your way to recovery. Pick an image that is particularly comforting to you for your personal journey. Imagine floating on water or strolling through the woods or along a peaceful path. Perhaps the journey will feel most comforting if it is just a relaxing walk through your own home.

Unexpected things will sometimes occur on your journey to recovery. You are learning many things that will help when you hit a trouble spot. You will be prepared for these possibilities.

Think about what you're learning. but don't worry about it. The learning is already taking place. Continue to think about your own recovery. You are learning coping strategies that will be useful as you move forward on your journey—strategies that will help you overcome your own particular roadblocks. Maybe you now have one or two ideas that have meaning for you but that you haven't learned how to use yet, or perhaps the most useful strategies are brand new to you. Now that you've begun the journey to recovery, continue to move forward and begin to focus on the satisfactions that await you, as you feel better and better.

Script 4: Mindful meditation for the body and the mind

Allow yourself to bring your attention to your breathing, taking a breath and noticing your breath as it moves in and out of your body . . . continue to focus on your breathing . . . take another breath . . . hold it . . . and let it go. Continue to gently focus your attention on your breath as the breath passes in and passes out again. Remain focused on this present moment. It doesn't matter whether you breathe in any specific way. Without any effort, your breath will be okay . . . your body knows how much air it needs . . . just begin to observe the in-breath and the out-breath . . . and when thoughts come in, notice these thoughts rising and passing away . . . no need to judge, just observe. When you become aware of your thoughts, gently bring your attention back to your breath . . . just be fully in this moment . . . without trying to make anything happen . . . using the breath as a point from which to observe thoughts which will inevitably come to mind . . . the urges, planning, memories, impatience which hinder our ability to just be in this moment . . . adopt a nonjudgmental attitude of acceptance . . . and when you become aware of these thoughts allow yourself to be with your breath. Notice any difference in the breath without trying to control it . . . just focusing on the current breath. If your thoughts wander, gently bring your attention back to the breathing, noting what that is like for you. Allow your breath to become slow and notice your body in the chair . . . how you are sitting . . . what your body feels like . . . perhaps gaining some sense of the room . . . allowing yourself to be in this moment . . . there is no right or wrong. Observe your thoughts as if they are on a stream traveling down the water . . . just noting the thoughts, and when you do, gently bring your attention back to the breath. When you are aware of judging or trying to control, observe the process and bring your attention back to your breath . . . there is no right or wrong way to

meditate . . . just bring your mind back to the breath when it wan-
ders knowing that it may wander hundreds of times . . . and each
time return back to the breath . . . without judging.

When you feel ready, begin to gradually bring yourself back to
the room . . . perhaps stretch your body . . . gain a sense of the
room . . . and then, slowly open your eyes . . . knowing that in
time you can bring on this state of appreciating and being in the
moment, observing your thoughts, developing a detachment from
your anxiety throughout the day.

Continue to practice for ten minutes, or expand the practice session to twenty minutes or more whenever you wish. Use this process of mindful meditation throughout the day, taking a mini-meditation break whenever you are stressed. Notice the effect as you learn to observe your scary thoughts without feeling a need to react to them or fear them, instead gently bringing your attention back to your breath.

Practice whichever relaxation exercises have the most positive impact for you as you continue your journey—the journey from worry and fear to recovery.

~ ~ ~

As you read these stories, you'll notice that each of the people who shared their experiences used breathing exercises successfully to help them relax in fearful or stressful situations.

Ronelle's story

In the seventh grade, I first started having panic attacks. Looking back, I can see that I had a lot of separation anxiety. I never wanted to stay overnight at friends' homes. As I got older, I was very conscious of my body and always worried about getting sick.

When the first panic attack occurred, I stayed out of school for a while. That was the time that I think I was the most agoraphobic. I had trouble even leaving the house. I was really afraid that something disastrous would happen to me physically, that I would die or have a heart attack or something else horrendous. As I started having more and more panic attacks, the idea that I was going crazy or would make a fool of myself in front of the whole class made me feel totally out of control. I started seeing a therapist, and between my mom and him, I eventually went back to school, but my problem continued to cycle up and down throughout my school years.

Going to college was a really big deal to me—I questioned whether or not I could do it. College was the first time I had ever left home, and it was a time when things got much worse. I went home quite often because, at that point, home was still a pretty safe place.

I had associated panic attacks with school, so I always thought that once I was out of school, I would be free, that the problem would go away. I wouldn't have the pressure to go somewhere every day. However, when I got out of college, the panic attacks didn't go away. When I started to think, "What am I going to do with my life?" my stress increased. I didn't have a clue about what I wanted to do. About a year after I graduated, when I started getting serious about my future, I started having trouble again. Things got as bad as I can ever remember. I began to worry about going crazy and never being able to function in life.

My heart rate was my main concern along with issues around breathing and not having enough air. I wasn't hyperventilating in the sense of having to breathe in a paper bag, but I've been told that I definitely hyperventilate without being aware of it. I would breathe way too fast and get a lot of weird body aches. I became depressed, convinced that nothing would ever change, and that I would never be normal. Finally, I got to the point where I thought, "I've got to find somebody who knows about panic!" I was very depressed and just couldn't deal with the attacks anymore. I felt nervous wherever I was— I didn't even feel safe at home any longer.

My mother, who I felt really close to, got some information for me, and I began to research the problem of panic and anxiety attacks. The turning point for me came when I finally found a specialist in panic disorder who could help me.

Learning how to breathe properly was the most important factor in my recovery. It was really powerful for me to know that my breathing was causing a lot of my symptoms. It was really cool to be able to focus on my breathing and get control. The idea that I'm in control and if the symptoms get worse, I can do something to feel better, was very important to me.

I had a lot of problems quieting my mind for the more complex relaxation skills, so I learned to sort of cue myself to relax. Practicing has helped even though I was convinced it wouldn't. I've been getting better gradually, and I've become a little more objective about the situation by reminding myself that my body is not doing the same thing my mind is thinking. Also, I look at what is really going on. "Is there really any danger? No, there isn't some horrible thing happening. Things are okay." It's been fascinating for me to learn that my body is doing the right thing, but the messages I'm sending it are wrong. Now I have developed the habit of just saying, "It's okay. I feel stressed and tense, but I don't need to panic."

I think at this point I've internalized a lot of what I've learned in counseling. Now I can recall on my own many of the thoughts that my therapist taught me. In the past, I used to lose all that learning and feel that I was going to fall apart and have the worst panic attack I'd ever had. But eventually, something new happened to me. I began to deal with these scary thoughts as they came up, trying to talk back to the thoughts. Now, I constantly remind myself that I really don't have any proof of disaster. When anxiety starts to arise, I tell myself that it's an old habit and that I know everything is going to be okay.

In my opinion, the most important step in recovery is to get help from people who are knowledgable about the problem and then really educate yourself about it. Knowing what is happening to you makes the sensations less terrifying. Worrying about what might happen was always the worst part. I was afraid of the scary ideas in my own head that had no basis in reality. Now I know that I was afraid of things I didn't need to be afraid of.

Jim's story

My first panic attack hit me in 1979, and it was a living hell. It came out of nowhere, hitting me at work one day. I got up from my desk right away and went outside the building for some fresh air. After a few minutes, I felt better, so I went back in, but the next day I had two or three more attacks while at work. The third day I didn't want to go back. Then the attacks began to spread, occurring at gas stations, shopping malls, stores, and restaurants. I'd get nauseated, very disoriented, and dizzy. My eyes would get blurry, and I couldn't even see my way to the door, so I'd sort of feel my way out. I'd start sweating and get cold and clammy while I was trying to get out of the building, and believe me, I would never go back. I thought I was losing my mind!

I gave up using credit cards when I wanted to buy something because they took too long to be processed. I used to go to happy hour with my girlfriend, but now I went only if she drew me a floor plan of the place with all the exits marked along with where we were going to sit. If the designated table wasn't free, we didn't go into the bar!

A doctor gave me tranquilizers, which I took for eight months, but the only thing I could do was drive to work and home. I didn't want to try anything. I slept from four in the afternoon until dinner and then went right back to bed. Sleep was my escape.

After doing some reading on the subject, I felt somewhat better, and I thought I was going to be able to handle my panic attacks, but when I got married and moved out of state, the attacks came back and were more intense than ever. The old symptoms returned, and I couldn't work. I was even having panic attacks at home. Totally overwhelmed, I called one of the local hospitals who referred me to a therapist.

This counselor showed me how to grade the intensity of my panic. That was helpful, because I always assumed that it was at its highest level. In reality, some attacks were less severe than others.

One night, I went to a pub with some friends. I was very anxious, but I did relaxation exercises and deep breathing in an attempt to calm myself. When I joined in the conversation around the table, the anxiety would rise again, but I did the relaxation again too. It wasn't comfortable at all. I either wanted to have a panic attack, or I wanted it to stop. At that point, I called my therapist, and she helped me understand that for the first time I was able to control my anxiety. Also, for the first time, I saw that making progress didn't mean I had to be 100 percent better. After that, everything started to improve. I could control the panic enough to give me the confidence to practice. Finally, I could go wherever I wanted to, a restaurant, a store, or a bank, and I could even stay there when it was most crowded.

Once, after a few months of counseling and then getting a job, I went to a restaurant to have lunch. I ended up staying there four hours because I was so happy to be in a restaurant and really enjoying it. It was such a high!

The panicky thoughts were the last thing to go. After the panic attacks were gone, the thoughts were still there. Now, I talk to myself and say, "You've been fine for a long time. If an attack comes again, you know what to do." I know I will never, never be as bad as I was before. That's because I know so much about panic now. I know the necessary steps to calm myself. To anyone who is suffering panic attacks, what I want to tell them is, "You can get better . . . and you are not alone."

Cognitive Techniques
for Overcoming Anxiety

*Thinking your way
to recovery*

As you continue on the road to recovery, begin to observe your levels of anxiety, rating them on a scale from 0 to 10. Notice that the levels are not constant. Your anxiety, in fact, goes up and down. It goes up when you are concentrating on your most frightening thoughts and bodily reactions. These peril predictions keep you tense and hypervigilant.

Listen carefully to the messages you are sending yourself about your symptoms. It may be very normal to experience some tension in certain situations, like having to give a speech or getting on an airplane. However, your own thoughts about possible danger can make the difference between an anxiety level of 1 or 2 in a specific situation and a level of 8 or 10 in that same situation.

If you predict that a catastrophe will occur or that you will be unable to cope or that you will need to escape or that something bad might happen if you don't worry and stay on guard, your anxious feelings will intensify. The "Frightened You" takes over. Increasingly alarming thoughts cause you to assume that anxiety automatically signals danger, no matter what the evidence.

Chances are, part of you believes that your anxiety is a response to a real threat in your life, even though another part wonders if this is true. It is understandable that you will have trouble relaxing if you believe that you need to be vigilant and

worried to protect yourself. You may have said to yourself—
"Don't worry, don't panic," many times. Others may have told you
to forget it, think of something else, don't overreact—but if you
really believe there is something to worry about, it's understandable
that you won't want to let down your guard.

Let's look at anxiety and panic in a new way—a way that will put
you in control.

Reassuring the Frightened You

Fortunately, there is another, more rational voice within you. The
Rational You guides you through life's events, evaluating the
relative safety and danger in each situation. This voice can reassure
and comfort you when you actually are safe.

In order to strengthen the Rational You, examine the specific
thoughts that increase your feelings of anxiety and begin to evaluate
the evidence for and against your concerns. This is called rational
responding, or de-catastrophizing.

Cues to anxious thoughts

Perhaps the boss doesn't say hello. You may see this as evidence that
he wants to fire you. In the same way, you can begin to interpret any
event as full of danger. If people don't smile, you may believe that
they think you are boring and that they don't want to be with you.
Or when your heart beats rapidly, you may think you could have a
heart attack, although these palpitations may have happened before
and medical tests show you to be in good health.

Almost any event, physical sensation, or image can provoke
worry, anxiety, or panic once the Frightened You takes over. Think
about a recent anxiety or panic attack and try to recall the thoughts
that went through your mind. Record them on the "Catching
Anxious Thoughts" worksheet. If you have difficulty identifying
your thoughts, try to imagine yourself in the anxious situation as if
you were in a movie. Review the scene in your mind and write down
your reactions.

Catching Anxious Thoughts

The last time I felt anxiety or panic, I thought _____

_____

_____

Take this book or some notepaper with you and catch the
anxious thoughts right after they occur. What are the most
important anxious messages you are telling yourself?

_____

_____

_____

_____

_____

Often the thoughts you are aware of represent only some of your
concerns about a situation. They are one link in a chain of related
fears. It is important to bring all the other thoughts into your
awareness, for often a deeper concern is driving the rest. Uncovering all the meanings will help you get to the heart of the matter.

Getting to the heart of the matter

Using the "Getting to the Heart of the Matter" worksheet on page
52, you will have the opportunity to consider one of your peril
predictions or anxious thoughts and to uncover all the levels of
threat that lie beneath your immediate fear.

You may not be aware of the specific danger messages you are
sending yourself. Sometimes it's too frightening to think beyond
your focus on uncomfortable physical sensations or the instinct to
flee, avoid, check, or procrastinate. Looking at all the consequences

of your peril predictions may be unfamiliar. As you practice the exercises in this book, you'll become more skilled at identifying these predictions of danger.

Before you begin filling in your own responses on the "Getting to the Heart of the Matter" worksheet, look at how Carol, David, and Kevin responded when asked if their peril prediction happened, what it would mean, and what would be so bad about that. Note that although they began with a specific fear about a specific situation, when they asked these questions of themselves again and again, they eventually recognized many other levels of threat.

Responses to the
"Getting to the Heart of the Matter" Worksheet

Carol predicts that she might have a panic attack when she shops alone and loses control.

And if that happens, she says: *"Everyone will see me losing control."*

And: *"People will wonder what's wrong with me. They won't want to assist me."*

And: *"No one will help me. I'll be stranded."*

And: *"I'll get so dizzy, I'll faint or I'll have a heart attack from my panic symptoms."*

And: *"That means I can't handle life on my own."*

David fears that if he feels tense in a restaurant, he'll start to shake, and people will notice.

And if that happens, he says: *"I'll feel humiliated. They'll think something is wrong with me."*

And: *"I'll get sick and faint. Then they'll have more proof that something is wrong with me."*

And: *"People will notice and comment. It will confirm my worst fears about myself."*

And: *"I'll never want to eat in a restaurant again. I can't take the chance."*

And: *"I can't allow anyone to see a weakness in me."*

Kevin worries that he won't finish his work project on time and his boss will notice.

And if that happens, he says: *"The boss will be disappointed in me. She'll wonder why she hired me in the first place."*

And: *"She'll realize I'm not as good as people think. She'll want to get rid of me."*

And: *"I'll lose my job. I won't have money."*

And: *"I'll never get another job as good as this one. My family will have to get by on very little."*

And: *"My family will be let down. They'll think of me as a terrible failure."*

And: *"Everyone will know that I'm incompetent."*

Now, on the "Getting to the Heart of the Matter" worksheet, write your own peril prediction. Then record what you fear might occur if your peril prediction came true. Next, respond to the question, "What would be so bad about that?" Continue on down the worksheet, asking yourself at each step, if the event immediately above happened, what might happen next. In your final statement, you may find that you have uncovered your deepest fear.

Getting to the Heart of the Matter

My peril prediction _____

_____

_____

If that occurs, what might happen next?	What would be so bad about that?
If that occurs, what might happen next?	What would be so bad about that?
If that occurs, what might happen next?	What would be so bad about that?
If that occurs, what might happen next?	What would be so bad about that?

Looking at the odds/looking at the danger

Now you have identified some of your peril predictions. It's crucial to understand that these predictions seem valid because they are associated with so much anxiety and fear. However, we encourage you to begin to view your predictions of peril as ideas rather than truths.

Without this crucial step, your thoughts can appear to be true just because you think them! However, as you begin seeing your thoughts as ideas that occur to you during anxious moments rather than as prophecies, you can begin to test your thinking and discard those frightening thoughts for which there is little or no evidence.

How do you question your thoughts? First note the specific events, images, or physical sensations—the cues associated with your fearful thoughts. Next identify your anxious thoughts, using additional copies of the "Getting to the Heart of the Matter" worksheet to list them.

Looking at the odds

It's common for people with anxiety problems to overestimate the likelihood of danger. The following exercise will help you gain evidence about how accurate your predictions are.

Picture one part of you, the Frightened You, giving all the evidence you feel supports your peril prediction occurring.

Next, allow the Rational You to gather any facts regarding the likelihood of your prediction not occurring.

The following questions will help you weigh the evidence for and against the likelihood of your prediction occurring. Then you can revise your prediction to reflect all your new information.

- Has the feared peril ever occurred?
- If so, how often, and what have been the consequences?
- How would someone else view this evidence?
- If the peril didn't occur, what do you think kept the feared event from happening?
- Are you taking all the information into account?
- How can you gather additional evidence?

Before completing the "Looking at the Odds" worksheet, read how several other people with anxiety problems evaluated the odds of their peril predictions happening.

Responses to the "Looking at the Odds: Strengthening the Rational You" Worksheet

Jeff looked at the odds of embarrassing himself while making a sales call.

a. Time: Wednesday

b. Anxiety cue: Sales call

c. Peril prediction: I'll start to sweat, and everyone will notice and think I'm incompetent.

d. Odds that this will occur (0-100%): 80%

e. Evidence for: When it happens, I feel humiliated. Sometimes people notice.

f. Evidence against: Even though I worry about it all the time, I have no evidence that my anxiety changes how people view me. I still make sales.

g. New odds of prediction occurring (0-100%): .001%

h. New self talk: It's true that I don't like sweating and appearing nervous. Even when I do sweat a lot, most of the time no one notices. Those few who do still think highly of me.

Barb looked at the odds of sustaining an injury while on a hike.

a. Time: Friday

b. Anxiety cue: Worrying about going hiking

c. Peril prediction: I could fall and break my leg on the top of the mountain, and we couldn't get help, and I could be injured for life.

---

d. Odds that this will occur (0-100%): 90%

e. Evidence for: Bad things happen, and we'd be stranded.

f. Evidence against: Hiking is a pretty safe activity, and hiking accidents are rare. We will stay on cleared and easy paths, and I'll wear the right shoes.

g. New odds of prediction occurring (0-100%): .001%

h. New self talk: I notice that I often overestimate the likelihood of accidents when I have to do an outdoor activity, and when I do things, accidents have never happened.

Karen looked at the odds of dying in a plane crash.

a. Time: Thursday

b. Anxiety cue: Reading in the paper about an airplane crash

c. Peril prediction: The plane I'm taking to the conference will crash.

d. Odds that this will occur (0-100%): 80%

e. Evidence for: I just feel it will happen to me.

f. Evidence against: Airplane travel is considered quite safe. In fact, the odds are one in ten million that a person will die in a plane crash.

g. New odds of prediction occurring (0-100%): Less than .000000001%

h. New self talk: Airplane crashes are scary for everyone, but the degree of risk is so small that I feel comfortable taking the chance. If I remind myself of the realistic odds, I will eventually be able to lower my anxiety when thinking about flying.

Paul looked at the odds of getting fired.

a. Time: All last evening

b. Anxiety cue: Tension and constant worry thoughts

c. Peril prediction: I'll never have enough time to do all I have to do tomorrow, and I'll let everyone down. My boss will think I can't do my job. He may fire me.

d. Odds that this will occur (0-100%): 75%

e. Evidence for: Everyday I make a list of what I have to do, and I never complete it, and I feel like a failure.

f. Evidence against: Even though I have trouble getting everything accomplished, my supervisor seems generally satisfied. I have never slacked off at work.

g. New odds of prediction occurring (0-100%): .01%

h. New self talk: I do have trouble organizing myself and sticking to one thing until it's completed. That makes it harder to feel satisfied at the end of the day. But my standards seem to be higher for myself than others expect of me. It is very unlikely that I will disappoint everyone when I don't do as much as I want to. If I work on time management skills I will be able to accomplish more.

Shelly looked at the odds of having a car accident.

a. Time: Friday

b. Anxiety cue: Having to drive to an unfamiliar restaurant

c. Peril prediction: If I panic on this unfamiliar road, I might have an accident.

d. Odds that this will occur (0-100%): 80%

e. Evidence for: I'm bad with directions and I just know it will happen.

f. Evidence against: I have been able to do more alone recently. My last few car trips alone have been okay. If I get lost, I can ask for directions and practice my breathing to calm down. Even when my anxiety is high, I've never had an accident in the car.

g. New odds of prediction occurring (0-100%): .00001%

h. New self talk: I am a safe driver and have never had an accident in the car, even when I have panicked. I am ready to practice on unfamiliar roads.

You have read how other people evaluated and rethought their peril predictions. Now it's time for you to complete the worksheet on the next page, "Looking at the Odds: Strengthening the Rational You." When you determine, after looking at the evidence, that the peril you fear is not very likely to occur, write new self-talk messages that you can use when you begin to feel anxious.

Looking at the Odds: Strengthening the Rational You

a. Day/time:

b. Anxiety cue (events/thoughts/sensations):

c. My peril prediction:

d. Odds that my peril prediction will occur (0–100%):

e. Evidence for the likelihood of my peril prediction occuring:

f. Evidence against the likelihood of my peril prediction occuring:

g. New odds that my peril prediction will occur (0-100%):

h. New self-talk after reviewing all the evidence:

Looking at the danger

Just as anxiety sufferers may overestimate the likelihood of danger, they may also overestimate the severity of the outcome if the feared event should occur. Picture the Frightened You giving all the evidence for how terrible it would be if your peril prediction occurred.

If you are predicting death or other extreme outcomes, of course the worst would be a calamity. If, however, you are predicting embarrassment or loss of control, employment or social opportunities, allow the Rational You to gather reality-based information on how you would cope with the feared outcome. Perhaps the worst is not as bad as you think. Even when the worst happens, people do recover, often discovering strengths and resources they never knew they had. Remember the amount of time you can feel anxious or stressed is limited and will pass.

On a 3″ x 5″ First Alert card, write your peril predictions on one side and your new ways of assessing risk based on evidence on the other side. Carry the card with you, and when you are plagued with catastrophic thoughts, use the card as a reminder to talk to yourself as objectively as you can. Ask yourself whether you have any evidence to support your thoughts that disaster might happen. Is there any other way you could view the situation or test your prediction? Think of any other ways you can give the Rational You the upper hand.

When the Frightened You takes over and anxious thoughts intrude, you can also try observing them and then gently refocusing your attention on the actual situation. Stay focused on what you are actually feeling now—"I feel my heart beating," for example, rather than, "I am going to have a heart attack." Stay attuned to the situation rather than to your fear of what may be about to happen.

People who develop anxiety reactions sometimes label every feeling they have as anxiety or stress. See if you can identify feelings other than fear or anxiety when you are experiencing discomfort. Perhaps you're excited, sad, lonely, angry, or disappointed. Ask yourself, "What would I be feeling right now if I weren't feeling anxious?"

Another way to say this is, "What else am I feeling underneath my fear?" If those other uncomfortable feelings are due to something other than anxiety, you may be able to work on solving the other problems, or you may need to accept some of those feelings as normal parts of being alive.

Differentiating anxiety from fatigue, hunger, or a physical response to caffeine, heat, or humidity can reduce the potential anxiety problems. You may have become reluctant to feel intense emotions, instead becoming anxious when you have reason to feel sad or angry. The more you begin to identify and get comfortable with your entire range of emotions, the less scary and more manageable all your emotions will become.

Before you begin the "Looking at the Danger: Strengthening the Rational You" worksheet, read how other people who struggle with anxiety evaluated the actual danger if their peril prediction happened. After they considered all the evidence, they usually reduced the danger rating substantially.

Responses to the "Looking at the Danger: Strengthening the Rational You" Worksheet

Jeff looked at the danger if he embarrassed himself on a sales call.

a. Time: Wednesday evening

b. Anxiety cue: Sales call

c. Peril prediction: I'll start to sweat, and everyone will notice and think I'm incompetent.

d. Danger rating if the event occurs (0-100%): 100%

e. Evidence for: A salesman needs to be confident, and they'll see I'm not confident. I'll be so embarrassed. They won't place an order, and I'll lose my job. I won't be able to support my family.

f. Evidence against: Even when I sweat, I certainly have no evidence that they think less of me. I close the deal most of the time whether it happens or not.

g. New danger rating (0-100%): .001%

h. New self talk: It's true that I don't like appearing nervous to others, but most of the time it doesn't occur, and when it does, it is uncomfortable but not a disaster. People don't think less of me, and they still do business with me. I'm not going to lose my job because of this.

Barb looked at the danger if she were to have an accident while hiking.

a. Time: Friday

b. Anxiety cue: Worrying about going hiking

c. Peril prediction: I could fall and break my leg on the top of the mountain, and we couldn't get help, and I could be injured for life.

d. Danger rating if the event occurs (0-100%): 95%

e. Evidence for: I would have to lie there until help came, and I might not get to a doctor in time to prevent permanent damage.

f. Evidence against: There will be other hikers to come to our aid if we need help. Even in the highly unlikely event of a serious injury, it probably wouldn't be life-threatening, and I could cope.

g. New danger rating (0-100%): 25%

h. New self talk: When I do things outdoors, accidents have never happened. If I did injure myself, it either could be minor, or we would figure out a way to get help. I could cope in the unlikely event that I had an accident. I need to focus on the odds more.

Karen looks at the danger if the plane she is on crashes.

a. Time: Thursday

b. Anxiety cue: Reading in the paper about an airplane crash

c. Peril prediction: The plane I'm taking to the conference will crash.

d. Danger rating if the event occurs (0-100%): 100%

e. Evidence for: Most people do die in crashes.

f. Evidence against: I could escape, but an accident would be dangerous. Instead, I need to focus on the odds of a commercial flight crashing, which are extremely small.

g. New danger rating (0-100%): 90% but the likelihood is very small.

h. New self talk: Airplane crashes are scary for everyone, but the degree of risk is so small that I can allow myself to become more relaxed on flights. If I remind myself of the realistic odds, I can learn to think about flying without a lot of distress.

Paul looked at the danger if he were fired.

a. Time: All last evening

b. Anxiety cue: Tension and constant worry thoughts

c. Peril prediction: I'll never have enough time to do all I have to do tomorrow, and I'll let everyone down. My boss will think I can't do my job. He may fire me.

d. Danger rating if the event occurs (0-100%): 80%

e. Evidence for: If I get fired, I'll never find another job, and I'll be a total failure.

f. Evidence against: My boss comments positively about my work. I could cope with the unlikely possibility of getting fired. It would be painful, but I have the ability to get another job.

g. New danger rating (0-100%): 10%

h. New self talk: I have no reason to feel my boss will fire me, but I could even cope with that if I had to. I do have skills and can survive.

Shelly looked at the danger if she has a car accident.

a. Time: Friday

b. Anxiety cue: Having to drive to an unfamiliar restaurant

c. Peril prediction: If I panic on this unfamiliar road, I might have an accident.

d. Danger rating if the event occurs (0-100%): 100%

e. Evidence for: I might die in the accident.

f. Evidence against: I've panicked, but I always recover. Nothing worse happens. I will be uncomfortable, but that doesn't mean I'll have an accident.

g. New danger rating (0-100%): 100% if it happens, but the likelihood is very small.

h. New self talk: I am catastrophizing because of my panic attacks. While driving has been uncomfortable, I do not have accidents. I'm a very safe driver.

You have read how other people reevaluated the changes they would face if their peril prediction came to pass. On the "Looking at the Danger: Strengthening the Rational You" worksheet, you can take a good look at your own predictions of catastrophe, reassess the danger, and write some realistic and supportive statements that you can use to reduce anxiety.

Looking at the Danger: Strengthening the Rational You

a. Day/time:

b. Anxiety cues (events/thoughts/sensations):

c. My peril prediction:

d. Danger severity rating (0–100%):

e. Evidence for catastrophe if my peril prediction happens:

f. Evidence against catastrophe if my peril prediction happens:

g. New danger severity rating (0-100%):

h. New self-talk after reviewing all the evidence:

Catastrophic thoughts and rational responses

Practice evaluating the odds and danger of all your peril predictions. If you do this every time you begin to become anxious, you will strengthen the Rational You. Review the catastrophic thoughts and rational responses below. Revise them to fit your situation, write them on First Alert cards, and carry them with you.

1. Catastrophic thought: "I always panic or have too much anxiety when . . . "

   Rational response: "Even though I feel like I could have a panic or anxiety attack, I may be overestimating how often they occur. When I look at past situations, I don't always have anxiety or panic attacks, even when I worry about the what if's."

2. Catastrophic thought: "I know I'll have a heart attack or stroke."

   Rational response: "These body sensations are uncomfortable, but not dangerous. My body is merely reacting to my fears."

3. Catastrophic thought: "People will notice how embarrassed I am."

   Rational response: "So what if people notice I'm embarrassed. Most people won't notice, and those who do may be understanding and helpful. If not, I can still cope."

4. Catastrophic thought: "I'll be trapped."

   Rational response: "I have options."

5. Catastrophic thought: "I'll lose control and act foolishly."

   Rational response: "I feel confused and uncomfortable, but I have never lost control. Even if I did look foolish, how bad would that really be?"

6. Catastrophic thought: "I'll be embarrassed if I start to hyperventilate."

   Rational response: "It may not happen. But, if it does, I'll remember to take slow, gentle breaths. I have no evidence that anyone notices."

7. Catastrophic thought: "What if I do panic?"

   Rational response: "If I panic, I can tolerate the distress like I have in the past. I'll remember that panic is time limited and not dangerous."

8. Catastrophic thought: "What if my child is kidnapped at school?"

   Rational response: "The real chances of that happening are extremely low—my child is safe."

9. Catastrophic thought: "I'll never have enough time to accomplish what I want to."

   Rational response: "I can use my time more effectively if I stay focused and calm and remember to use my time management skills."

10. Catastrophic thought: "Every time I think of flying, I panic. I'm never going to be able to fly."

    Rational response: "I am conditioned to feel panic when I think of flying. These feelings are not predictors of my ability to recover from my flying phobia. I need to practice the exercises in this book and then take flights until I'm no longer frightened."

Looking at your assumptions

Many of our thoughts spring from basic beliefs about ourselves, especially, and about others as well. These beliefs usually develop in childhood and are very deeply ingrained. If unexamined, these beliefs may cause you to dismiss or discount the Rational You.

You now have plenty of evidence about when your anxieties are false alarms. Yet, if you are having problems relaxing and letting go of excess anxiety, pay attention to when your ingrained assumptions are holding you back. Some of the basic rules you follow in life may be setting up expectations for yourself or others that are impossible to meet. Your ingrained assumptions about yourself may keep you stuck and unable to tap into your full capabilities.

On the following pages, you will read some common ingrained assumptions which are associated with anxiety problems. Are any of these assumptions getting in your way?

As you look at each assumption, ask yourself "To what degree do I believe that this statement is true of me." Rate your beliefs on the following scale: 0 = not at all, 1 = a little bit, 2 = quite a bit, 3 = extremely.

Perfectionism

____ I feel a constant pressure to achieve.

____ I criticize myself when my performance isn't perfect.

____ I rarely feel I've done enough no matter how hard I try.

____ I often give up pleasure in order to be the best at every-thing I do.

Control

____ I have to be perfectly in control at all times.

____ I worry about how I appear to others when I am anxious.

____ I feel that any lack of control is a sign of weakness or failure.

____ I don't feel safe if I allow someone else to take control of a situation.

People pleasing

____ My self-esteem depends on everyone else's opinion of me.

____ I will do things I'd rather not do so others will like me.

____ I am better at caring for others than caring for myself.

____ I keep most negative feelings inside to avoid displeasing others.

Competence

_____ I believe that I can never do as good a job as other people.

_____ I believe that my judgment is poor.

_____ I believe that I lack common sense.

_____ I feel like an imposter when I am told my work is good.

Responsibility

_____ I must always be there for others.

_____ If I look weak, I'll be letting everyone down.

_____ No matter how stressed and overloaded I feel, I have to do whatever I am asked.

_____ I shouldn't ask for help no matter how much I need it.

_____ I have to fulfill the needs of other people before I take care of myself.

_____ If I don't worry about everyone, I'm not doing my job, and it will be my fault if something bad happens.

Dependence

_____ I feel unable to manage on my own.

_____ I need to have people help me or be around when I'm anxious.

_____ I need a lot of reassurance from others.

_____ I see myself as a dependent and helpless person.

Undesirability

_____ I am socially inferior.

_____ If people knew how uncomfortable I feel, they would not want to be with me.

_____ I'm unattractive and turn people off.

_____ I'm uninteresting and have nothing to say.

_____ If anyone sees any sign of my anxiety, they'll know how defective I really am.

If you rated your belief at a 2 or a 3 on some of these statements, it is possible that these beliefs have become roadblocks to your recovery. For example, if you believe, "I have to be perfectly calm at all times," you may be burdened with a lot of extra tension in your life. No one is calm all the time! These assumptions add stress and make you more vulnerable to anxiety and panic. Be aware that these beliefs are a deeply rooted part of you. You may be surprised at how many of your actions are the result of these assumptions and how much they interfere with your desire to reduce anxiety.

The first step to altering these beliefs is to notice the impact they have on your anxiety level. Discuss your beliefs with a therapist or friend to gain more perspective.

After you recognize these troublesome beliefs, you have choices. You can try different experiments. For example, you can try acting in a way that is opposite to the way you usually behave. Then, evaluate the results. If you are a people-pleaser and have a difficult time showing anger, try something new for you. Tell someone you know that you are upset and see what happens.

If you need to be perfect to feel worthwhile, choose to do less than your absolute best and notice the consequences. For example, if you're taking a class and have to write an essay, try this experiment—choose to write a "B" or a "C" paper this time. Don't even try to write the "A+" paper that you would prefer.

Observe yourself when you are trying to be perfect and in total control, when you need to always be responsible or to please people, when you have feelings of incompetence, undesirability, or helplessness. Allow the Rational You to use this awareness to reevaluate your beliefs and gradually remove some excess pressure from your life.

~ ~ ~

*In the stories that follow, you will read about people who used
cognitive techniques to help them become more rational about evaluating the odds of their peril prediction happening.*

Nancy's story

I had a terrible dread of becoming sick and throwing up. In first
grade, a classmate got sick, and it really bothered me. The only
incident I can recall that I can trace this fear to was a visit I made with
my mother to a friend's home. Somehow my mother communi-
cated some kind of disapproval or embarrassment that affected me.
That's not to lay the blame on my mother—it's just that I was
impressionable. In the years that followed, I was afraid that I might
get sick, and I was also very nervous around other people, thinking
that they might get sick.

In elementary school, the rambunctious boys wanted to race to
see who could drink their milk the fastest. I hated that, and I hated
lunch hour. Also, I always wanted to sit near the door of the
classroom, so I could escape to the rest room if necessary. These
fears continued all through high school and college.

As an adult, the problems got worse when I was under stress. I
went through a divorce, and it really got bad. I could only eat at
home. Restaurants have always been a constant source of problems
for me.

I suffered from the stress of the problem and from the stress of
hiding it from everybody. If I got asked out, first I'd think, "How
am I going to deal with it if I get sick?"

Once I had a particularly bad business trip. I was with a group
of people, and someone got the flu. Even though I wasn't sick, I got
into a panic, and the whole trip was unbearable. After I got home,
I felt like I couldn't deal with my anxiety any longer. I'm talking
about twenty-nine years of having this problem. I decided that it
was about time I solved it.

I started therapy, and it helped me get my scary thoughts under control. I began to say things like, "Okay, what would happen if you actually became sick?" That made me realize that I was more concerned about the embarrassment, the public humiliation, than anything. The next step was to say, "Well, you could live through getting sick, so what?" It didn't seem so catastrophic when I began to see things in a new way. It wasn't as if I woke up one day and said, "Wow, I'm cured!" It took awhile to change my behavior and then awhile longer for all the new thoughts to really sink in.

Now if I'm feeling vulnerable, I'll say, "What's the worst thing that can happen?" It's important to know how to reassure yourself. The worst part about having panic attacks is being so embarrassed about it. Shame can really get in the way of recovery. Reading books about panic helped because I realized I wasn't that unusual. I found out that a lot of people have panic attacks and about weirder things than I have. Things I was so mortified about that I wouldn't even talk about them are not so unusual. Now I consider myself a normal person. It was hard trying to hide this deep, dark secret. It's a relief to have all that in the past.

Charlie's story

I am president and chief executive officer of a large corporation. About five years ago, I began finding myself in situations where I would feel very hot and clammy and sweaty. If I was with people in a one-on-one situation, I would feel very nervous and anxious, perspire a lot, notice that I was perspiring a lot, and then escalate and catastrophize the situation to make it even worse—a real cycle of sweating and worrying. This would eventually cause me to try and escape from the situation by leaving or moving around. Eventually I began avoiding social situations that I feared would put me in this state of mind.

All of this began because of my job, which has very high social demands—cocktail parties, speeches, panels, and the like. I began having problems in cocktail party situations, then occasionally when I was giving a speech. It got so bad that even sitting in church with large groups of people made me very anxious, and I would start to perspire. Eventually I found that going to a supermarket and standing in line was also a problem.

Initially, I simply avoided the situations that made me uncomfortable. I began slowing down my lifestyle. I quit going to church, tried not to attend social functions, and stopped giving as many speeches.

But, I could not avoid all social situations. After one anxious evening, I was so frustrated with myself I decided that perhaps I would break down and use a program that I had started for my employees, an Employee Assistance Program. I called a therapist, thinking that one or two visits would be beneficial and would somehow take care of me. I thought that perhaps I needed some medication or something.

I did go ahead and get a physical, which showed that there was absolutely nothing wrong with me. I had already tried having a couple of drinks before a social situation, thinking that perhaps the alcohol would help. I was very fortunate in that it did not help because if it had, I might have pursued that as a solution.

During my counseling sessions, my therapist and I really began to get at the roots of my problem. I had put myself in an overstressed condition. I was just working way too hard and finding no time for myself. I had not developed any techniques for pressure relief that would allow me to sit back, think, and reflect. So the first thing I had to do was deal with stress reduction. The second part was to really analyze what was driving some of these thoughts. I tended to be very much a perfectionist and to have a critical eye towards things and people. I was able to trace this back somewhat to my upbringing. Looking back, although I didn't realize it at the time, I can see that I had very critical parents. "Stand up straight," "Fix your shirt," "Do this-do that." So, I had to relax the sense of perfectionism I had ingrained in me.

Finally, I also had a sense of worry—real sense that I could lose my job and find myself pushing a shopping cart around town and being homeless. I was not good at rational thinking about my fate. So, one of my other tasks was to begin to pick apart some of my overdramatic thinking and really think realistically. I got good results once I was able to ask myself, "What basis of fact do I have for thinking that this is truly a problem?"

I have found it very helpful to confront myself with questions like that every day, following the questions with realistic affirmations.

Ed's story

I was often very anxious. I had difficulty in crowds and difficulty being with people. I would perspire, feel uncomfortable, become anxious, and my heart would pound. I felt very uneasy and uncomfortable.

My career has gone very well. In the course of eight years, I had four promotions. But because I had this problem, I always wondered if I would be exposed or discovered.

When I was in charge of meetings, it was getting the meeting started that caused me to feel uncomfortable. I felt insecure and not in command of what I was doing. Once the meeting got under way, I usually was okay, but I still felt that everyone was focused on me and that something I did would probably be wrong. I felt that people were looking at me, and I worried about my own inner feelings instead of thinking about the situation.

I was very frustrated. It was easier if people came into my office because that was my territory and I could control it better, but sometimes I would look at my calendar for the day and just not even want to go in to work. I could see that it would be one confrontation after another. My sick days increased, which was unusual for me.

I felt as though I was a fraud even though I wasn't. I wondered if I really belonged in this position, at a fairly young age, with a lot of responsibility. I worried that everyone would discover that I was inadequate or incapable of doing the job or less qualified than my subordinates. I believed that future promotions would not be given to me, although that proved to be totally inaccurate.

It took me some time, but eventually I did recover. One of the things I had to do was not try to be all things to all people. I cut back on stress on the job and the number of meetings I attended—things like that. Stress management helped a good deal. I began focusing on what I was doing instead of on myself. That helped, and now I feel much better. I still experience a few butterflies, but when I think about the fact that I have prepared well and have some good things to say, I can focus on the situation instead of my feelings. I am working my way back.

Learning to Face
Situations I Fear

Exposure techniques for
overcoming avoidance

We have given you tension reduction and breathing exercises as well as ways to challenge your peril predictions; the final step in breaking free from your anxiety or panic is to expose yourself to what you fear using your new skills as resources. Before you begin practicing this technique, list the situations, sensations, and thoughts you either try to avoid or can't get out of your mind.

You may find that what you fear most is what is often with you—the internal sensations your body produces when you perceive that you are in danger. Approaching what you are afraid of means approaching your feelings of anxiety. In a courageous and deliberate step, you may actually increase your sense of anxiety in order to learn how to manage it. It is important to remember this when you practice exposure.

Your security moves

When you experience anxiety or panic, you may adopt a variety of strategies in order to avert disaster. You may attempt to avoid the situation; you may focus extensively on it; or you may try to distract yourself. We call these maneuvers "security moves." Although they make you feel temporarily safe, you need to let go of these security moves as you learn to face the situations you fear.

Some of these security moves can be very subtle so much a part of your reaction that you're not even aware you're making them. But when you use one of these strategies and the danger you had predicted doesn't occur, you have the feeling, often without being aware of having it, that your security move saved you. This encourages you to practice the same strategy again. Unfortunately, it does not free you from fear.

The role of avoidance—a type of security move—is complex. It is responsible for perpetuating your fear of certain places because the longer you avoid a place, the more likely it is that you will begin to believe that avoidance is what's keeping your fears under control. So the longer you avoid a place, the harder it becomes to go there again.

By avoiding specific places, you are attempting to avoid the frightening sensations and thoughts you predict you will experience. By trying to eliminate the sensations of anxiety or panic at all costs, your fear of having these feelings ultimately intensifies.

Rather than trying to avoid a situation, you may focus intensely on what you fear, even if doing that frightens you more! If you have an airplane phobia and read about all the airplane crashes, or if you worry about your family's safety and constantly examine the news for disaster, you are paying a lot of attention to what can go wrong in life. This attentional focus reinforces your sense that the world is an uncontrollable place and that catastrophes are highly probable.

A third kind of security move involves trying to escape from your physical sensations by distracting yourself. Trying not to feel those things associated with the onset of panic or anxiety, you may pretend to be elsewhere or you may perform repetitious tasks unrelated to the situation. You may fight to stay completely in control by "white-knuckling," or tensing. While these strategies may allow you to carry on with your routine, they may also reinforce your fears.

Your security moves are reinforced because when you use them, they often lower your anxiety at that particular moment. For example, if you believe you must leave a social gathering when you feel anxious, you may always stay near an exit so it will be easy to flee. If you do this, you will end up believing that by remaining near an exit, you're actually keeping yourself safe. Or if you often check to make sure a loved one is not in danger, and if doing that makes you feel less anxious, then it's easy to think that checking often is what keeps the loved one safe. If you believe that, it will be hard not to keep checking. Who would want to take the chance of something bad happening just because you didn't stay vigilant?

Security moves look like they avert danger, but the price is very high: they reinforce your belief that there is something to be afraid of. Each time you leave a situation before your anxiety begins to show; or each time you take someone along because you think you might faint and need their assistance; or each time you cancel your flight because you think the plane might crash, you feel better temporarily, but the fear remains.

The most successful way to reverse this process is to gradually let go of your security moves. Facing what you fear means entering situations you would prefer to avoid, without distracting yourself; letting go of excessive checking, worrying, or procrastinating; and above all allowing yourself to experience the full range of fearful thoughts and body sensations. This takes a lot of courage. However, using the new coping skills you are acquiring will enable you to test your beliefs about the danger. In the process, you will discover that you have strengths and abilities you previously did not recognize, and this will enhance your self-confidence.

In the paragraphs that follow, you will read how other people challenged their security moves and faced their fears. The consequences that followed for them were not dangerous, and the benefits gave them freedom and confidence.

| **Kevin wrote:** | I had stopped exercising in order to avoid feeling my heart beat faster, even though my doctor had told me I'm in good health. |
| Challenge | I began to exercise and experience any physical sensations that might follow. |

Consequences	I felt a little anxious but nothing worse happened.
Benefits	Now, I can resume exercising. The physical sensations are to be expected and are harmless.

Barbara wrote:	I ate only soft food in restaurants to avoid having trouble swallowing.
Challenge	I ordered a sandwich.
Consequences	I practiced relaxation exercises before eating to relax my muscles. I didn't choke or die.
Benefits	Now I can eat a normal variety of food. I know that I'm not in any danger when I order whatever I want.

Chuck wrote:	I always sat near the exit in movie theaters so I could leave quickly.
Challenge	I chose a seat in the center of a row.
Consequences	My anxiety went up, but I practiced my coping strategies and was okay.
Benefits	Now I can sit anywhere I want. I just need to get used to it and challenge any peril predictions.

Maria wrote:	I usually wore very light clothing to avoid feeling warm and sweaty and having people notice.
Challenge	I wore a sweater and turned the heat up.
Consequences	I felt warm and sweaty, but no one else seemed to notice.
Benefits	Now that I know I'm more aware of sweating than anyone else is, I don't need to prepare for something that doesn't matter.

Dan wrote:	When writing a report, I repeatedly checked the time to see whether I had enough time left.
Challenge	I allowed myself adequate time to complete the report and didn't check the clock until it was done.
Consequences	I became tense at first, but I was able to complete the report on time—maybe faster than usual.

Benefits   Now, I'll allow what seems to be enough time and not spend that time on checking the clock.

Now you can begin to fill out the "Security Moves" worksheet on the next page. Complete the first column, listing as many of your own security moves as possible. If you have difficulty doing this, think about the times you predicted dangerous outcomes that didn't materialize. What did you do to prevent the outcome that you had feared? Next, begin to plan a strategy for challenging each of your security moves and record these strategies in column two.

As you continue through this chapter, learning how to challenge your fears by exposing yourself to them, you will be able to complete this worksheet. Starting with the least threatening situation and supporting yourself with the coping strategies that you are learning, you will be able to begin eliminating your security moves, one at a time. The third column of this worksheet gives you a place to describe each episode. Reviewing this record of achievement will give you the confidence to continue. To encourage yourself, you may want to list in the fourth column the benefits you will receive when you no longer need your security moves.

You may feel ready to begin eliminating some of your security moves immediately, supporting yourself by using the relaxation processes you have been practicing along with the new self-talk you have been developing. If you don't feel ready quite yet, you will find that the exposure techniques that are described in this chapter will be very helpful to you. You will learn, for instance, that you can begin to confront your fears in your imagination. That can be a first step toward actually entering the situation you fear without using your security moves.

Security Moves

Security move	Challenge strategy	What happened	Benefits for the future

The exposure process

Now we will take a detailed look at how you can gradually, in a step-by-step process, expose yourself to situations that you fear. First, you will learn how to expose yourself in your imagination to anxiety-related situations. Next, because you may fear your own physical sensations, you will learn how to induce the sensations you fear. Finally, you will begin exposing yourself to your fears in real life situations. You will benefit from some or all of these exercises, but in order to get full benefit from them, regular practice is essential.

We encourage you to explain to your primary care doctor what you will be doing. You may want to bring this book along to help you describe these techniques, which may sound very unusual, but which are being used in research centers around the world.

Before you begin the process of exposure, list the situations that make you feel anxious and rate the intensity of the fear they produce. In the paragraphs that follow, you will read how other people rated their situations. Then you will have the opportunity to do the same for yourself.

Responses to the
"Exposure List" Worksheet

Mark lists physical sensations and thoughts or images as well as events and activities as producing anxiety.

Others may think something is wrong with me.	8-9
Fears of someone hurting me.	9
Losing control, "going crazy."	9
Worrying about the death of a loved one.	10
Being totally alone through death, disaster, etc.	10
Driving out of my neighborhood.	9
Driving up hills.	10
Feeling a knot in my stomach.	7

Sharon's need to be perfect and in total control of her life is made clear by her list.

Not being able to take care of myself.	10
Imagining being homeless.	10
Worrying about not doing a good enough job.	7
Too much to do—not enough time to do it— muscles tense up.	7
Not getting the job done in the time expected.	8
Having an anxiety attack.	10
Financial ruin.	10
Having to live with my parents and start over.	7

Jennifer is extremely conscious of her physical sensations, which, in themselves, are frightening.

Feeling weak, light-headed, shaky, panicky, hot, and feverish, generally ill.	10
Severe intestinal distress before going out, sufficient that I cancel plans.	10
Significant intestinal distress before going out or intestinal cramps while out.	8
Light-headedness, inability to think well, feeling out of control, shaky.	7
Nausea, shaky.	7
Moderate intestinal distress.	5
Feeling spacey, not right, fearful that worse symptoms will develop.	5
Self-conscious, overly aware of all body sensations. Edgy.	5
Mildly uneasy.	3

Matt fears other people's reactions to his nervousness. He believes that people will think less of him if they know about his anxiety.

Sitting in a middle of a pew at church.	9
Sweating at a meeting and not being able to leave.	10
Talking to people at a party and feeling trapped, wondering if they'll notice I'm nervous.	8
Giving a talk.	8
Having an associate say something bad about me.	8
Feeling like I'm going to start to sweat.	7
Suddenly sweaty.	9
Picturing myself trying to hold a conversation and not be able to speak.	10

Jennifer's list is focused on her specific phobia, the fear of flying.

Imagining myself on an airplane.	10
Hearing about a plane crash on the news.	9
My husband getting upset because I won't fly to Wisconsin for family events.	8
Buying tickets for a flight.	8
Boarding the plane.	9
Takeoff.	10
Turbulence.	10
Landing—I haven't flown in 20 years.	10

Now that you have read how other people rated their anxiety in specific situations, and before you begin to practice exposing yourself to that which you fear, complete the "Exposure List" worksheet on the next page, listing the situations, sensations, and thoughts you either try to avoid or can't get out of your mind and rate each according to the intensity of your feelings.

You will refer to this list as you begin using the techniques on the following pages to recover from panic and anxiety. At first, you will

Exposure List

List situations, thoughts or images, and physical sensations you
are anxious or worried about, or which may cause panic, then
write a number from 0 to 10 that represents the intensity of your
feelings.

Situations, thoughts, and   Anxiety or
physical sensations   panic rating

_____   _____

_____   _____

_____

_____   _____

_____

_____   _____

_____

_____   _____

_____

_____   _____

_____

_____   _____

_____

_____   _____

expose yourself to situations that produce low levels of anxiety. With practice, and as you experience success, you will feel ready to challenge the situations that you fear the most.

Regard your first attempts as ways to explore your present limits. Try not to be too hard on yourself or discouraged if you experience difficulty. It took a long time for your fears to become firmly established, and it will take time and practice for them to subside.

Exposure in imagination

Imagination is very powerful, and you can use it as an ally in your recovery. Using your imagination in a controlled manner and repeatedly picturing yourself experiencing your fear will in time help reduce it. Over time, you'll start to get used to that which you fear. This process also gives you an opportunity to get to the heart of the matter—exposing yourself to your peril predictions in your imagination while letting go of your security moves. You will then be able to practice and strengthen your coping skills in real life situations.

You will be able to try a variety of exposure-in-imagination exercises. We will first describe an exercise in which you focus on your anxiety and next imagine yourself using your coping skills while in the anxiety-producing scene. If you have trouble reentering a situation in which you've been very anxious or panicked, try this exercise.

Imagine yourself back in the situation—attending a party, giving a talk, taking a flight, allowing a loved one to engage in an activity that is actually safe but about which you worry, entering a shopping mall or restaurant—choose a situation that you fear. Review those parts of the experience that make you most nervous, recalling your physical sensations and thoughts.

As you notice your anxiety begin to rise, begin using your slow, gentle breathing. Picture the Rational You reassuring the Frightened You as you remain in the situation. Keep the scene in your mind as you continue to practice your coping skills. Notice your fear diminish; experience a feeling of success. Repeat this exercise frequently until you begin to feel comfortable with the process.

You can role-play the scene with another person, using props to make the exposure contain as many fear cues as possible.

As you are now aware, avoidance maintains your fear. Directly facing the worst outcomes that you can imagine may be very unpleasant, but it will help you develop a more objective view, become less frightened about distressing thoughts and sensations, and stop worrying that there's something worse out there.

The "Exposure in Imagination" worksheet on the next page will guide you in writing an anxiety scenario that will fully expose you to all levels of your fears. Begin by choosing one of your lower rated anxiety items. You completed this form back in the chapter "Cognitive Techniques for Overcoming Anxiety," but this time, take your peril prediction to its worst possible conclusion.

After you complete your anxiety scenario, read through it, focusing on the worst aspects of your peril prediction. Rate your anxiety level from 0 to 10 and continue to deliberately bring on your anxiety until it is at a moderate to high level. Once your anxiety level is high, spend an additional ten minutes focusing on the situation, imagining yourself living it, really being in it. Keep focused on the most frightening elements in the scene. Looking at this worst vision, keep reading your scenario to maximize your anxiety.

Resist the urge to use any of your security moves. For the moment, try not to avoid your anxiety or distract yourself. Stay with the feelings of discomfort. If you find yourself wanting to hold back, continue anyway. Sometimes, closing your eyes, listening to a audiotape of your scenario or trying some other variation may increase your anxiety. You might tense your muscles, overbreathe, or attempt to produce other associated physical sensations to make the scene more present. During this part of the experience, you are trying to induce and increase your anxiety, not control or reduce it.

After ten minutes have passed, take a slow, gentle breath and begin to use the coping skills you have learned in this book. Keep your peril prediction image in your mind and allow the Rational

Exposure in Imagination

My peril prediction _____

_____

_____

If that occurs, what might happen next?	What would be so bad about that?
If that occurs, what might happen next?	What would be so bad about that?
If that occurs, what might happen next?	What would be so bad about that?
If that occurs, what might happen next?	What would be so bad about that?

You to weigh the evidence for and against the likelihood of the peril happening and how bad it would be if it did. As you continue to use your slow, gentle breathing, allow the Rational You to sift through the evidence and generate alternate views about your peril prediction. The Rational You will help you discover less threatening perspectives that you can recall in the future. Keep using your coping responses until you can rate your anxiety level at a level of 2 or below. Allow at least twenty-five minutes for this part of the exercise. Repeat this exposure in imagination technique a number of times over a period of days until the scene provokes a less fearful response. Next, repeat this sequence with every item on your "Exposure List" worksheet, practicing from the least anxiety-provoking items to the most troublesome.

If you're having trouble activating anxiety in your imagination, you may be using a security move such as distraction. It is understandable that this exercise might seem scary; however, you need to imagine yourself fully in the scene and allow yourself to experience your anxiety in order to test your beliefs. If you encounter difficulty lowering your anxiety after the exercise, perhaps the Rational You needs some assistance in generating less threatening alternatives. Before you continue, review the chapter entitled "Cognitive Techniques for Overcoming Anxiety" in this book and discuss this issue with your therapist.

Exposure in imagination practice

In the next paragraphs, you'll read how Paul vividly imagined a situation that he feared, brought his anxiety to a high level, then used relaxation techniques and rational self-talk to reduce his anxiety. Then you'll have the opportunity to practice this technique yourself.

Paul suffers from stage fright, a phobia shared by many people. He began his exposure in imagination exercise by writing the following scenario:

"I walk up to the lectern. I'm giving a talk at work. As I begin to speak, my mouth gets dry, my heart starts pounding, I feel dizzy, and nothing comes out of my mouth. I want to run away, but I can't. I'm stuck on the stage. Everyone starts to laugh. I look in the audience and see my manager's face. He looks very angry and is shaking his fist at me. The laughter is so loud I hear it ringing in my ears. I'm humiliated. I'm also stuck on the stage. I can hear whispers and finally shouts from the audience—'Get off the stage, you jerk.' Someone throws an eraser at me. I'm completely humiliated. I'm now at a level 8 on my anxiety scale."

After writing this scenario, Paul imagined himself in the most feared part of the situation, allowing his anxiety to rise to level 8 as he had predicted. When he felt extremely tense and fearful for ten minutes, he began the next step: reducing the anxiety.

"I take a slow, gentle breath and notice that my neck and shoulders are stiff. As I exhale, I say 'relax' and focus on releasing tension from the stiff parts of my body. I begin to identify my peril prediction—that I'm going to freeze while giving a talk and totally humiliate myself—and look at the probability of it happening. At first I believe that the probability is 100%. The evidence for that prediction is that I do get very nervous when I give talks, in fact, I've avoided a few this month. The evidence against that prediction is that I've given hundreds of speeches and have always been able to talk, in fact, I'm usually complimented on my delivery. The anxiety usually stops when I get into my topic, but even when it remains, I never get negative feedback."

Paul has begun to recognize that his peril prediction probably won't happen. But he still must deal with the question of how serious the consequences would be if his prediction did happen.

"The consequences would be 100% severe if I panicked during a speech. I'd never be able to face everyone at work again. My family would starve, and we would all end up on the streets."

When Paul looked at the evidence against this severity rating, he wrote:

"I've coped with problems before and disaster hasn't struck.

People at work are pretty understanding, and my reviews are very good. I'd be embarrassed, but I'd get over it in time. If they fired me as a result, I would feel terrible at the time, but I have marketable skills and would be able to find work. I've never been fired and have always provided for my family. It's more realistic to rate the severity of consequences at 30%."

Then Paul wrote some new self-talk statements and an action plan on a First Alert card:

"I often get nervous while giving talks, but no one seems to notice my anxiety. I can perform well even while anxious, and my anxiety does decrease as I continue talking. I think I'll join a public speaking group and keep practicing how to reduce my anxiety."

Now that you've seen how Paul induced anxiety in his imagination, reduced it with relaxation and rational thinking, rethought the consequences of his peril prediction, and recorded his new self-talk, try this technique yourself. You will begin by describing, on paper, a recent anxiety or panic episode.

- First, write all the details—your thoughts, physical sensations, and actions—as vividly as possible. Even if nothing terrible really happened, take the episode to the worst conclusion that you fear.
- Next, record how this episode affected or might have affected you and others—again as vividly as possible. Keep asking yourself, "And if this happens, what would that mean?" "How bad would it be?" Use as many pages as necessary.
- Conclude by estimating, on a scale from 0 to 10, the level of anxiety this episode would produce.

When your scenario is complete, you will visualize the situation that you described, recreating the episode in your imagination. Before you do this, however, reread the previous pages of this chapter to remind yourself how to induce your feelings of panic or anxiety. If you have trouble making the visualization come alive, practice first by imagining a neutral scene, one that does not make you feel anxious. Imagine yourself standing in a grassy field, for example, hearing the sounds of birds, feeling the warmth of the sun on your face, touching soft petals and crisp grass. When you can vividly imagine this or a similar scene, you will find it easier to visualize an anxiety-producing situation.

Now it is time to begin exposing yourself in your imagination to the scenario that you described on paper.

- Begin by spending ten minutes imagining the worst parts of the episode, allowing your anxiety to rise to the level that you had predicted.

- Next, take a slow, gentle breath. Spend the next twenty-five minutes or more using all of the coping skills you've learned in this book. Keep your peril prediction scene in your mind and allow the Rational You to sort through the evidence and come up with alternative self-talk. Rate the severity of the consequences if your peril prediction were to happen, then examine the evidence and give the consequences a new rating.

- Write your thoughts and conclusions on the same page as you wrote the scenario.

- On a First Alert card, record any new perspectives and self-talk statements that you found to be particularly useful in reducing your anxiety.

As you continue to develop new First Alert cards, be sure to carry them with you. The insights, relaxation techniques, and self-talk statements on them are your first line of defense when you begin to feel anxiety or panic.

Sensory exercises

Another exposure strategy involves exposure to internal fear cues—rapid heartbeat, shortness of breath, blushing, sweating, etc. When anxious or panicked, you may not realize that your fear of your own body sensations is bringing on your anxiety; you might be so focused on your worried thoughts or on the dreaded situation that your fear of your own body sensations goes unrecognized.

Once you learn that your scary physical symptoms are really under your voluntary control, a change in your heartbeat or your breathing will no longer lead to a panic attack.

With the help of your therapist, these fears can be reduced. The following sensory exercises have been designed to produce sensations similar to the physical sensations you fear. With repeated practice, the sensation will remain but the fear will lessen or disappear. You will come to understand that these sensations, while uncomfortable, are not dangerous. The results of research studies on this technique, which has been evaluated primarily in relation to panic reduction, have been very positive. Listed below are several sensory exercises, each intended to produce a particular physical sensation:

- hyperventilate
- spin in a chair
- hold your breath
- shake your head from side to side
- run in place
- bend quickly, then straighten up
- rapidly run up and down stairs or step on and off a box
- put your head between your legs, then raise it suddenly

Add to this list any other physical activities that activate your sensation of fear. To select the most helpful exercises for you, try each of them. Again, your coping strategies will be very useful after your exposure session.

Sample all the exercises with your therapist for the recommended amount of time. Using the "Sensory Exercise" worksheet on the following page, describe the intensity of each sensation, the intensity of your anxiety or fear, and how much the sensation resembles what you feel when you are anxious. For example, how well do these feelings duplicate the sweating, flushing, or dizziness you may feel at a social gathering or the hyperventilation that begins during a panic attack? Next, choose the exercises that produce the

Sensory Exercise (after medical clearance)

Add to the list of exercises below any others that trigger physical sensations similar to those that you fear. On a scale from 1 to 10, rate each sensation's intensity, then the intensity of the anxiety it provokes. On the next line, describe how this sensation relates to what you feel during anxiety.

Intensity of
Sensation / Anxiety

1. Hyperventilate (30 sec.)   _____   _____

   _____

2. Spin in a chair (1 min.)   _____   _____

   _____

3. Hold your breath (30 sec.)   _____   _____

   _____

4. Shake your head from side to side (30 sec.) _____   _____

   _____

5. Run in place (30 sec.)   _____   _____

   _____

6. Bend quickly, then straighten up (30 sec.)   _____   _____

   _____

7. Rapidly run up and down stairs (30 sec.)   _____   _____

   _____

8. Put head between legs, then raise it (30 sec.) _____ _____

   _____

                                                _____   _____

   _____

                                                _____   _____

   _____

sensations that most resemble your anxiety or panic. Rank those exercises from least to most anxiety-provoking.

Start with your lowest ranked exercise. Once the uncomfortable sensations begin, continue the activity for at least thirty seconds (hold your breath, however, for only ten seconds). Try to produce the strongest sensations possible, focusing your attention on those sensations without distraction. Then stop and rate the maximum level of anxiety you experienced. Follow each experience with slow, gentle breathing. Notice any peril predictions that the Frightened You is producing. Let the Rational You weigh the evidence and produce alternative, less threatening views.

Continue using your coping strategies until your anxiety level is reduced to a rating of 2 or less. At that point, repeat the sensory exercise you are using in the same manner as before. Repeat this sequence in its entirety until the fear produced during the exercise is at a rating of 2 or less, practicing up to five times daily. Work your way up the list of sensory exercises until you can cope with even those that induce the most anxiety.

You will discover as you continue that you can experience the physical sensations without experiencing the fear. This exercise increases your ability to view familiar, but distressing, sensations as safe, not dangerous. Be patient, if your progress is slow, spend as many days as you need on each exercise.

Real life exposure

Now you are ready to test in daily life all that you've learned. Return to the "Exposure List" worksheet on page 84. Review your list and add any other items that come to mind. Begin your practice with items having lower anxiety ratings and then move to more feared situations.

Once you begin to experience some success, it will be easier for you to continue on to more difficult situations. But note: how you define success is very important. If you assume that every practice session has to be perfect or that there is no way you could cope in a certain situation or that practicing once is enough, your standards are too high. That means that it will be very difficult for you to feel good about what you are doing. In the beginning, success might be that you are able to maintain a 7 or an 8 on your anxiety scale, rather than a 10. Give yourself credit for what you accomplish in small steps! Maintaining an anxiety level of 7 or 8 or watching the level rise and fall without escaping, is real progress.

Practicing these exercises will give you real proof that anxiety, while uncomfortable, will not make your worst fears come true.

You will begin by reentering the situations that you find least frightening. Or you will reduce your checking under the least threatening conditions. Gradually you will build up to more challenging circumstances.

At first, try to identify what tends to raise your anxiety level. Then see which coping strategies are most helpful for you. Remember: the goal is to face and tolerate some anxiety without escaping from the situation. Although you can escape a feared situation at any time, if you leave while your anxiety level is high, it's best to return and reenter the situation as soon as you can get more practice.

If you fear your physical sensations and tend to avoid or suffer through situations where you experience these sensations, practice as you did with the sensory exercises listed on page 92. Use real life situations that evoke similar feelings such as crowded, poorly ventilated rooms, sex, lifting heavy objects, listening to the news, getting angry, drinking caffeinated beverages, etc.

If you have any trouble getting back into a situation in which you've been anxious on a previous occasion, break the task of going back into small steps. For example, if you've had a bad time in elevators, you might just want to look at the elevator on the first try, and the next time press the buttons to call the elevator, and later actually get on the elevator. For other people, getting on the elevator right away seems to work best. Going with a partner you trust or a therapist may also help you.

If you avoid giving talks, you might want to join a support group and practice there. Move on to a more difficult environment after you gain confidence.

If you feel self-conscious at social gatherings because of sweating, you could begin by jogging until you perspire and then going into a store for exposure to a group of people. After that, attend the least frightening gathering on your list. Be prepared to use your coping skills. If you avoid flying, you could begin by watching the planes land and take off, and then book a flight, and only later actually board a flight.

Remember that when you escape or run away from a fearful situation, the anxiety grows in your mind, and it will be much harder for you to enter that situation again. So, if you can, rather than leave, pause . . . wait . . . breathe. Often your anxiety will subside.

When you are planning an exposure session, view it as a situation that has three phases:

1. Preparing for the symptoms before they occur,

2. Coping with the symptoms when they occur, and

3. Reinforcing yourself for coping, and staying with the situation —taking pride in the step you've accomplished.

During the preparation phase, remember that coping techniques such as slow, gentle breathing, relaxation, and rational thinking will help you look at yourself and your symptoms more positively, in addition to preparing you for the actual situation. For many people, the anticipation is much worse than the actual situation itself, and these techniques can really decrease your worry about the "what if's."

When you are in the fearful situation, you'll be testing and practicing different skills, learning how effective they are for you. Measure your decreasing anxiety levels to discover which techniques are the most useful for you, and rely on these techniques in the future. Keep your First Alert cards handy. Use them for support and record new information on them.

If you feel discomfort in the situation, whatever it is, you have a chance to deal with it. Face the internal sensations you fear. Experiencing anxiety will help you realize you can tolerate it and you can continue with your life. You know you can tolerate a lot of anxiety because you already have! Even severe anxiety episodes can teach you that catastrophes don't happen just because of the way you feel. There's a very good chance that you've underestimated your ability to withstand and cope with anxiety.

It's important to acknowledge your success. Give yourself a pat on the back for trying. Success might simply be allowing yourself to remain in the situation and experience the physical sensations of anxiety, knowing that these sensations will eventually fade away. Then you will see that staying in the situation will decrease rather than increase your anxiety. When you experience this, you will have achieved a major breakthrough.

During these practice sessions, even the smallest steps are progress. One sign of progress is learning to notice reductions in your anxiety while you are in a tense situation. This will happen when you stay in the situation, practicing slow, gentle breathing, and allowing the Rational You to evaluate the actual danger. Using all the strategies you've listed on your First Alert cards, you will experience ever decreasing levels of anxiety as you truly begin to believe that you will be okay and that worrying doesn't keep disasters from happening—it just overburdens you.

Every time you experience a success, record it on a small piece of paper and put it into an empty glass jar. Watch the jar fill up with your accomplishments. When you feel discouraged, empty the jar and read about each victory. Just looking at the jar can remind you of your progress.

Keep an exposure journal

If you keep a record of the exposure situations you put yourself in during your practice sessions as well as the level of your anxiety and the state of your thinking, you will have important information about what helps you the most. If you monitor your anxiety before, during, and after an exposure session, you'll notice that the level of your anxiety before you enter the situation in no way predicts the degree of anxiety you'll feel in that situation. Also, it doesn't predict how well you'll cope with your feelings. If you keep a record, it will be visual proof of your improvement. If you have a bad day or a setback, reviewing your records can help you maintain a better perspective and remind you that it's not a catastrophe. You are having ups and downs, just like everyone else.

When you are about to begin an exposure session or when you experience a frightening physical sensation, keep these ideas in mind. We have summarized many of them on the "Exposure Strategy List," on the following page. This list has also been printed in the back of this book. Clip it out and carry it with you for quick reference when you're feeling anxious and uncomfortable.

Now you are ready to test what you have learned. In your exposure journal, record details about the exposure exercises you try. After exposing yourself to the item on your exposure list that causes the least anxiety, record the following: What was the experience like? What did you learn? If you encountered roadblocks, problem solve how you can handle the next exposure.

Now return to your "Exposure List." Select the item next most severe in intensity. Use this three-step process:

1. Prepare yourself.

2. Cope with the symptoms.

3. Reinforce yourself for staying with the situation.

Then record the results in your exposure journal.

As you gain control over anxiety, a number of changes will take place. You will be able to focus more easily on those parts of the situation that are enjoyable or comforting to you. You'll begin to realize that the catastrophes you have been expecting don't really happen as you feared. If your fear returns at any point, you will understand it and know that you can handle it. You will learn that you can begin to function in situations even while you're feeling some level of fear, and you'll be able to appreciate that achievement.

Once your anxiety and panic attacks occur less often and your self-confidence increases, you will feel free to participate in activities you once avoided. At that point, you can examine other areas in your

Exposure Strategy List

1. Anxiety sensations are exaggerations of normal physical reactions and not harmful.

2. Worry is not a predictor of outcome.

3. Focus on the Rational You. Don't allow the Frightened You to take over.

4. Tell yourself, "I can enter my exposure session without my false security moves and be safe."

5. Practice your slow, gentle breathing.

6. Some anxiety is normal and to be expected.

7. Progress is gradual—recovery takes time. Be patient with yourself.

8. Focus on what is really happening to you and around you—not what you fear might happen.

9. Wait for your fear to decrease and notice when it begins to fade. If you leave an exposure session because of fear, return as soon as possible to continue practice.

10. Each practice situation is an opportunity to test your peril predictions.

11. Celebrate your successes, no matter how small. They will add up.

life that may have contributed to your distress. Were you at a crisis point when your anxiety problem developed? Investigating the kinds of thoughts or situations that preceded your anxiety problem may shed light on conflicts and tensions you can now begin to work on.

Try to identify other areas of your life that cause stress. If you're feeling trapped or uncomfortable in a relationship, now may be the time to look at what's troubling you. If you find that you are keeping your anger to yourself in personal relationships, assertiveness training might help you learn to let people know how you feel.

As you progress, you may find that your success in facing and overcoming anxiety will lead to more options in your life. Some of your relationships may need to be redefined. As your confidence grows, working on other areas of your life will become more possible.

As you read these pages, as much as you want to overcome your anxiety or panic, you may feel discouraged about the possibilities of succeeding. These thoughts are very understandable. But many, many others have succeeded—now it's your turn. We encourage you to begin your program for recovery right away!

~ ~ ~

For encouragement, read the following stories of other people's recovery to learn how they successfully recovered after exposing themselves to the situations that they feared. You can do this too.

Cheryl's story

I was in a movie theater when my first panic attack hit me. I started to get up at the end of the film, and a terrible feeling came over me. I felt like I was going to faint or die or something. When I got home, the dizziness didn't go away for a couple days. My doctor took some tests, but they all came back negative, so he said it was probably a panic attack. A few weeks later, I started having trouble going to sleep because I felt like I was choking. It was like I had a big lump in my throat, and I felt dizzy even when I was lying down. It was really scary.

Next, problems started when I was driving. I got dizzy on the way to work and on the way to the beauty shop, and my throat got tight. I felt pretty good all day while I was working, but many times I wanted to run out of the office and just go home. My family kept saying, "Just hang in there. If you go home, you're going to feel even worse."

Then I began to see a counselor, and I found out that I had actually been avoiding escalators for twenty years! I would walk up a flight of stairs instead of taking the escalator, afraid that I might fall off. The counselor went into the stores with me and showed me breathing exercises and how to get back on the escalator. I kept talking to myself, telling myself that people don't fall off escalators so there's really no danger of that. There can be a normal fear when you hesitate to get on, but that doesn't mean you're going to fall. Eventually, I was able to get on the escalator by myself.

I used the same techniques of breathing and talking to myself to get over my fear of driving. Now, in fact, I do most of the driving when I go with other women to square dancing and other activities. If I feel my anxiety begin to rise, I start the breathing exercises, and by talking to myself I can convince myself that everything is okay.

Sometimes I still have a little trouble sleeping, but I've even been able to work around that. I just get up and read a book instead of lying there thinking about panic. I feel like I'm really doing great now. I used to be afraid of so many things, but now I feel that I'm living again. I think I've come a long way.

Randy's story

I have fears of entering elevators, driving through tunnels, and flying. The tremendous fear of going through tunnels developed because I was afraid the tunnels would collapse. About twelve years ago, I had to attend a seminar in New York. I was given a room on the thirty-third floor. Being that high bothered me, and I also feared taking the elevators to get up there. They were very small elevators and very confining. The room itself seemed like a box. The windows couldn't even be opened. I spent most of the night down in the lobby talking to the hotel staff. I got very nervous and wanted to leave and go home. I couldn't fly home so I took the train.

As a result, I hadn't flown anywhere in twenty years.

Finally, I decided I had to do something about my fears. My daughter had moved to Washington and we wanted to visit her. Even though my wife preferred flying, we drove, and I found a way to avoid the Baltimore Tunnel by crossing a bridge. This trip became the last straw that spurred me to get help so I could get over these difficulties. I went to a therapist, and together we started going to an elevator nearby that went up five floors. First, I entered with the therapist, and then I began to go by myself.

I discovered that the first thing I did when I entered an elevator was to look at the indicator showing which floor we were on. I wanted to know how fast I could get out—I was looking for an escape. Instead of concentrating on getting out, I was encouraged to focus on feeling comfortable in the elevator and realizing I was safe there. So that's what I did. Now when I go into an elevator, I don't worry about it stalling or breaking down. If I do get a momentary twinge of anxiety, I can settle down, because I know that nothing terrible will happen.

Next my wife and I began to go through tunnels. We started at times when the tunnel would be less crowded and worked up to peak traffic times. Taking slow breaths from my belly, rather than from my chest, helped a great deal. I began to breathe as if I were blowing through a straw—slowly and gently. The breathing was a big factor in allowing me to manage my fear. Now there are many other relaxation techniques that I use automatically.

The first few times that I entered them, the tunnels were frightening! But as I drove through them, I overcame that fright just by confronting it. The belly breathing and listening to a comforting tape were helpful while I was going through the tunnel, and before I knew it, I had made it all the way. One day, driving back from Washington, we took a different route and headed into a tunnel I didn't know was there. I didn't tell my wife, but my anxiety level was about a 5 or 6 right before we entered the tunnel. However, there was no alternative but to go through it, so I used my breathing techniques and settled down. I knew I was panicking because the tunnel was unfamiliar, and I wasn't ready for it. But I drove through it and I was okay, so I realized I didn't need to be frightened of tunnels anymore.

I had done so well with elevators and tunnels that the therapist and I decided to take a shuttle flight from Boston to New York. I was afraid, but I was also determined to do it! On the way to the airport I was very nervous, but when I saw the plane, I imagined myself being inside and unafraid. It also helped to visualize the pilot and the big windows in the cockpit. I had a tranquilizer in my pocket, but I didn't take it. I didn't even order a drink. However, talking with the therapist helped as we approached the terminal and while we were on the plane.

What bothered me the most about being in the plane was the fact that they were going to close the doors. I knew I would feel extra confined when the doors closed. My therapist said, "You really wouldn't want the doors to be open when you were flying, would you?" That really got to me. That would be no way to fly! So, I immediately settled down and started doing my gentle breathing. Not only did I actually enjoy the flight, I felt accomplishment.

Later I discovered that flying is very exciting to me. I actually love the takeoff and I also like to land! I realize that my deepest fear was that I would panic and run up and down the aisle, totally out of control, like a crazy person. Finally I became convinced that I wouldn't really do that. I've flown many times since then. We have flown to see my daughter a number of times now. I fly whenever I can, my wife flies with me, and we both love it! My advice to other people is not to worry too much about panicking. If a panicky thought comes to your mind, immediately be sure you're breathing properly and change to a positive, more realistic thought. The most important thing I can say is, whatever you're afraid of, if you want to do it, *just do it!*

Claudia's story

I first started experiencing panic symptoms in 1976, and for a couple of years, I had no idea what was wrong with me. I was initially told by my doctor that I had a virus, and I kept waiting for the virus to go away. Every so often it would occur to me that maybe there was some psychological component in what was happening. Although I thought I would have had the education to accept that, it was very hard for me to think about. I kept insisting to myself that it was some kind of physical illness.

The worst symptom was the feeling that I was going to faint. I would feel extremely light-headed and became scared of passing out. I would hyperventilate. During the first really bad panic attack, I was hyperventilating to the point where my arms and legs were shaking. I was out of control. I had to breath into a paper bag to reestablish my carbon dioxide levels or whatever breathing into a paper bag does.

It was very hard for me to go places. Over the next fifteen years or so, I became better able to go places, but I still experienced quite a bit of anticipatory anxiety, most often in the form of intestinal upset, diarrhea, and cramps, what I would call "intestinal mambo." During the next few years, I was managing a lot better but only by curtailing where I went. I had the ability to be functional in a relatively limited geographic area. If there were days that I just could not get out the door to go to the swimming pool, which was seven miles away, nobody suffered for that except myself for not getting exercise.

But then I read an article about some advances that had been made in cognitive treatment that included doing things in a therapist's office that would bring on some of the symptoms of panic. It sounded like a very powerful technique, so I checked into where I could get that kind of treatment and started attending an anxiety management group.

I found this cognitive work to be very powerful. All of the techniques I had tried earlier involved distracting myself if I was feeling symptoms and doing things to keep my mind off the symptoms. For instance, it was very common for me, if I was driving and feeling symptoms, to keep singing to myself. What was different about this new cognitive approach was that, rather than distract myself when I feel symptoms, there are a series of questions that I ask myself to identify what am I thinking. For instance, if I am driving and start to feel a little anxious, I ask myself, "What am I afraid of? What am I most afraid of? Am I going to pass out? Well, have I ever passed out while driving? No, never. How many times have I driven? Thousands of times. Okay, what does that make the probability." I keep my rational statistician voice saying things like that instead of thinking, "Oh I am really scared. I am going to pass out." The statistician tells that voice, "I drive all the time. Sometimes I feel sick, but I have never passed out. What really is the probability? If I really did feel awful, how severe is that? It is not fun, but is it really life-threatening in any way? No." That kind of talking to myself has been the most powerful technique for me to use.

As a result of group therapy, if something happens in my life, I now take a look at why I get so upset and the underlying assumptions that might be making me so upset about one incident or another. For example, in the group, we completed a questionnaire about different ways that we see ourselves. It was paradoxical to me that I thought of myself as a very independent person, and yet I responded to some questions with the statement that I needed a lot of guidance. I told the group that was totally unlike me. I have an enormous amount of initiative. I had to ask why a very independent person would check the items about feeling dependent.

When I was a kid, I felt that I was a weak person when I was sick. I needed to prove that I was as strong as the other kids. If I was not, I felt that there was something deeply wrong with me. If I did get sick away from home, my fear was that I would have to have someone help me, a stranger maybe. I couldn't imagine doing that. The stranger would have thought badly of me. I think there is something inside me that made that assumption that they wouldn't help me, that I would die.

I did a little dialogue with myself, asking myself why I believed I was dependent. I learned that it comes from childhood messages, and that now I am an independent and resourceful person. The part that still feels dependent has probably played a big role in my anxiety symptoms.

Why Am I Having
Panic and Anxiety Attacks Again?

How to manage setbacks

Many people who have learned to handle their panic and anxiety attacks believe they are now "home free." When another attack occurs, it can be very upsetting and discouraging. When you have a setback, your disappointment can make your feelings of panic, anxiety, or worry seem even more out of control. Though you have made progress and are on the way to recovery, it may seem as if you're back to square one. The old pattern reasserts itself and your confidence may be shaken; you may once again become anxious about your anxiety or fearful about your fear.

However, setbacks are a natural part of the process of overcoming anxiety reactions. They can only happen if forward progress has already been made. They are normal, predictable, and can be managed. So, as much as you dislike them, expect that setbacks may occur as part of your progress.

When you experience a setback, it will be helpful for you to stop and assess your reactions so that you can get back on track during these frustrating, but inevitable, times. Let's look at what setbacks are, how they happen, and what you can do about them.

Why do I have setbacks?

Everyone experiences setbacks at one time or another. You will know you're moving ahead in your recovery when you are able to experience fluctuations in anxiety and worry without panicking and without losing your connection to your newly improved self.

Setbacks can happen for many reasons, but one may be that you set very high standards for yourself, possibly higher than anyone could achieve. If you believe you need to do everything as perfectly as you can, then even a small setback can easily seem like a catastrophe.

If you believe you must always control your anxiety and that you have failed when you can't, the setback cycle is perpetuated. The "should's" and the "have-to's" press in on you. You may think, "I might scream and make a fool of myself right here in front of everybody. I'll never be able to control my worry. I must have been wrong about getting over my anxiety—and after all my hard work."

Automatically the Frightened You focuses on the worst possible outcome. It is easy to once again exaggerate the likelihood and severity of danger; however, you can learn to recognize these responses, to again use all the strategies that have helped you, and to turn the setback into another piece of evidence that your worst fears don't happen.

The triggers of setbacks vary. Most often, they are part of the process of discarding old patterns of worry or fear and learning to have faith in the new, more Rational You.

Tension in relationships with your family and friends can sometimes be a cause of setbacks. When you first begin to feel better, you may discover that you behave with new independence and self-confidence. Your goals or expectations for yourself and for your relationships may shift. You may begin to be more direct with people about your needs and feelings. These changes may surprise you and those around you, and some friction may occur while everyone adapts. Sometimes a third party can help you gain a new perspective on changing relationships. Don't be afraid to consult a trusted friend, spiritual leader, or professional counselor.

Breaking free from the setback cycle

The setback cycle is a closed circle—it can go around and around, gaining momentum as you feel worse and worse. You can break free of this painful repetition by remembering that you now have choices. This will help you move from feeling helpless to feeling in control. A setback is a stressful but powerful learning opportunity. Ask yourself, "What can I learn from this experience? What can I learn about myself and my life that can push me forward in my recovery and make me stronger in the future?" Reread your First Alert cards. Don't focus on your setback. It is time for you to break free of your setback and reenter the recovery cycle!

The recovery cycle

The recovery cycle offers many options, choices, and paths for personal growth. Begin to transform your fear and discomfort into an opportunity!

Even if, after a setback, your anxiety feels at its worst, the understanding and knowledge you have gained about yourself and about ways to break free from anxiety will position you to move forward once again.

Think in terms of small successes. If you've ever watched someone learn how to ski, you know that it's a process of small successes. No one expects to do it perfectly the first time. In fact, falling down is an important part of learning how to ski. Learning to deal with anxiety reactions is a similar process. Each "failure" can teach you what to do differently next time. If you expect that a setback may occur, you can label the experience as an opportunity to gain information to use in the future.

Here are some common myths about setbacks. Compare them to the facts.

Myths about setbacks	Facts about setbacks
1. Setbacks are a sign of failure.	Setbacks are not my fault. They are normal, to be expected, and a part of recovery.
2. Setbacks mean I have to start all over.	I have already learned many anxiety management

strategies. It will take less time and effort to start using them again. I do not have to start all over again.

3. Setbacks mean I'm never going to get better.

Setbacks are signs of improvement. A setback can only come after an advance. That means I have made progress.

4. Setbacks mean the worst panic or anxiety attack will come back and never leave.

Setbacks are only temporary occurrences. I can gain increasing control over my anxiety.

5. There is nothing good about a setback.

Setbacks are opportunities to learn to manage anxiety in new ways.

6. Setbacks mean I'm abnormal, that I'm hopeless.

Setbacks are proof that I'm normal and that my progress to recovery is occurring. No one can master new skills without falling down and getting back up.

Steps to take during setbacks

Imagine yourself in a situation that makes you anxious. You're beginning to worry that your anxiety will escalate into an anxiety or panic attack. What can you do? Here are several very important suggestions:

1. *Challenge your thoughts.* What evidence do you have that your setback means failure? What proof is there that you can't succeed? The Frightened You can feel guilt, fear, frustration, and loss of self-confidence. The Rational You can review your previous progress and provide you with a more balanced

perspective. Remember that occasional failures are part of the growth process!

2. *Prepare for setbacks.* Expect them to occur. Accept that some circumstances will cause you excessive anxiety. Plan ahead, thinking about what you will do about a setback before it happens. Use the situation to practice coping techniques and strengthen the Rational You. Look at your First Alert cards for specific strategies that have helped in the past.

3. *Practice for success.* Choose your response to a setback; you can do that right now. Then you'll feel prepared to manage a setback when it happens and to use the setback as an opportunity to learn about yourself and how you can cope with stressful situations. A positive approach makes setbacks easier to manage and reduces the chance of future setbacks.

4. *Talk to yourself.* Pretend that you are talking to your best friend. Admit that you're having a rough time. Remind yourself that you've made progress and that the setback problem is temporary. Talk to yourself in a soothing, comforting voice: "Could I be overreacting? What's really happening? What kinds of peril predictions am I having about the situation?" The more you can identify your feelings, the more control you will have over them!

5. *Sort out what you are really feeling.* Other feelings, such as anger, sadness, or loneliness can be mistaken for anxiety. Perhaps something you're not even aware of is bothering you. Since many people have setbacks during stressful periods, try to identify any factors that might be increasing your vulnerability to increased anxiety. And don't forget to consider physical factors such as lack of sleep. Above all, don't blame yourself for whatever you are feeling; focus on the external circumstances that may be causing you to feel this way.

6. *Try to do some problem solving.* Reread this book. Use the practice forms. Begin by rating your anxiety. Identify what happened just before your anxiety level began to rise. Perhaps

you're only slightly uncomfortable, but you're worried that the level you're feeling right now, maybe a 3, might escalate into an 8. Stop, take a step back, and think. Your problem-solving efforts will teach you to recognize what causes your own setbacks. Then you can develop a plan of action to deal with these new discoveries. And you can remind yourself that competence breeds confidence.

7. *Review the records of your progress.* Your records are the visible proof of your progress. When you have a setback, look at those records; they'll remind you that you made it through these difficult times before and you can do it again.

8. *Stay active.* Don't allow a setback to disrupt your progress. But pace yourself. No one can tell you how quickly your problems will be solved. Allow yourself to experience all the anxiety-producing sensations, places, or thoughts as soon as you can. Practice coping strategies that have worked in the past.

9. *Get support from friends, family, or a therapist.* Share your feelings of frustration and disappointment with those who care or have special expertise with anxiety.

10. *Remember that these setbacks can be overcome.* Many, many others have succeeded, and so can you!

A new attitude about setbacks

Setbacks are natural. They are to be expected. As much as we all would like it, there is no such thing as a perfectly problem-free recovery. You've already begun the process, and you have many reasons to be proud of yourself. You are learning to view yourself as one who can cope. Now you can learn to replace your frightened definition of a setback with a more realistic understanding. As you progress, setbacks will occur less often, and you will begin to recognize them as minor disturbances, part of the normal ups and downs of living. And when you accept some anxiety in life as manageable, you'll handle these occasions more easily than ever.

~ ~ ~

Pam and George both recognize that occasional anxiety is normal and to be expected. They are able to avoid major setbacks because they don't panic when they become slightly anxious. Instead, they use coping skills that they have learned. They both feel confident that they will always be able to manage occasional anxiety problems.

Pam's story

The thought that I was a perfectionist never occurred to me because nothing I did was perfect! In fact, the flaws, mistakes, goofs, or whatever were always glaringly apparent, at least to me. Every time something wasn't right, I thought, "THEY will see and THEY will know." I don't know who "they" were, and I don't know why I cared so much about what others thought. I do know that my dad told me I could do anything if I wanted to do it bad enough, so somehow I guess I thought imperfections meant I hadn't tried hard enough.

I had reached a point in my life where I was doing a lot of things and always trying to do more. Mentally, I felt like I could do anything, but my body started sending me signals that said, "Hey, wait a minute. Not so fast." But since I believed that my mind should control my body, I really didn't even listen. And when I started getting weird physical sensations, like feeling that my head was in a vise or getting dizzy and seeing spots in front of my eyes, I thought I must have some kind of exotic illness.

Finally, on an out-of-town business trip, I went completely out of control. I was afraid of absolutely everything. I couldn't eat or sleep, and when I got up to give a speech, as I'd done so many times before, I just froze. My whole body went rigid. After that, the only thing I could think of to do was to force myself to try to stay in control of everything and always be on guard, prepared for the worst. After all, I thought, if I can't perform at 100 percent in my job, I will get kicked out and never asked back.

Back home, my family doctor examined me and then suggested I see a therapist. I was absolutely shocked! It took most of the

summer for me to get up the courage to go see one, but my
symptoms just kept getting worse and worse. Then I talked to a
couple of friends who shared some really important things with me.
One told me about her experience with fear after almost dying from
pneumonia, and her symptoms sounded a lot like what I was going
through. The other friend told me about her struggle with panic
attacks, which frankly I had hardly even heard of before. Then she
said, "If you really want to get well, leave no stone unturned." I'll
never forget those words. I went home and dialed the therapist for
an appointment.

Sometimes what I learned from the therapist still amazes me.
How could I have missed the fact that I had this huge amount of
"shoulds." I *should* look good, I *should* always do my best at every
moment, I *should* always be on time and never make a mistake and
be energetic and happy. And above all, I *should* be able to do it all
at once, all the time. I took these "shoulds" very seriously, so if my
husband and I were going to have a dinner party, I would go into an
incredibly high gear, making sure the food would be perfect, the
house spotless, even the kids' rooms upstairs! Then, there was such
enormous tension in my body during these events that the physical
fatigue was unbelievable! But, as I said, it still amazes me that I had
to learn that I didn't have to do all this and that I had to learn it from
a objective outsider, a therapist.

I began practicing physical relaxation, especially walking outside, slowly and freely—kind of like ambling. Then I started
practicing *not* doing certain things. Once I even had company over
without vacuuming! Not one person seemed to notice, so I pointed
out my "dirty" carpet, and they still couldn't see anything wrong. I
discovered that I was the one who was putting the pressure on
myself. No one else made the "to do" list but me.

I continued therapy for about six months and some really
encouraging things happened along the way. My behavior was
changing in positive ways and was being noticed by other people.
My husband commented about how much more human I seemed
to be, and that freed him up to be much more open and free with

me. People I had known for many years said it appeared that I was going through some sort of spiritual transformation—a beautiful awakening of my soul.

I don't have real panic attacks anymore, although I still have anxiety now and then, but I accept that as okay. After all, I keep reminding myself, I'm human—I'm not perfect. The real key is learning that you are creating the anxiety and panic attacks yourself, and in the end, only you can get yourself out. Attacks aren't something to be ashamed of; they are something to be worked through and overcome.

You know, I wouldn't have chosen to go through all the pain and suffering I have. However, I'm not sure I would be feeling as satisfied and good about myself as I do now if I hadn't had this experience and then learned to work through it. Can you believe it? I'm now one of the people on the other side!

George's story

When I was in high school I started having real problems leaving the city, whether to go on vacation or on business travel. I worried about it. I started anticipating it and fantasizing about all the bad things that could happen to me—getting sick, getting hurt, not sleeping, becoming embarrassed in uncomfortable situations. It affected me to the point that, in college, I would not go on ski trips or take vacations with classmates, not even trips to Mexico and things of that sort. I didn't go to parties where I would be out all night because I was too afraid that I was going to get hurt or get sick. I had a lot of problems with insomnia. I would not go on trips, or I'd make excuses not to go because I was afraid I would get insomnia on the trip, and the consequences of that would be that I would get sick from lack of sleep. When I was short on sleep, I would get sick for a week or two—sometimes three weeks. That would be very embarrassing because everybody else I knew was not like that.

I remember going to Disneyland. I tripped out—getting scared and really negatively fantasizing about the rides, having to go to the bathroom, and getting sick. I was making my own life miserable by what I was putting into it and by the type of thoughts that I had. They were not positive at all. They were entirely negative.

I had periods during which I could not go to work. I'd spend the whole day fighting fear, fighting off tears, and breaking into cold sweats. Finally, I started counseling and began taking an antidepressant. I think the therapy and medication both helped a great deal. I am very, very happy overall with my life now compared to just about any previous time.

It helps when I remain aware of my tension level, knowing that I can live with a certain amount of tension and recognizing that it does fluctuate. The tension is reduced by my thoughts, breathing, exercises, and acceptance. What I have learned is that nothing is 100 percent perfect. When I look at life this way, then life seems perfect! Whatever happens, happens. It's okay. Things could be better, things could be worse, but I continue to look at the big picture.

Before, I would really get upset if things got out of place around the house. I would let the house get out of hand, and then when I got to the point where it just completely looked the opposite of the way I wanted it to, I would get upset. The last couple of years have been great—like night and day compared to the previous years. Now I am pretty much relaxed about the way I live.

How Family and Friends Can Help

Do's and don'ts for those who care

Some of your family and friends may understand your anxiety problems and react with support and compassion. Others may appear bewildered and just not understand.

You may have tried to hide your anxiety problems from others for fear you would be judged or misunderstood. It is easy for excessive worry or avoidance patterns to create difficulties in your relationships and contribute to your stress. Just as you can feel frustrated, helpless, resentful, confused, and even angry when anxiety seems to get the better of you, people around you can feel equally strongly about the impact of your anxiety on their lives.

Often, however, all that family and friends really want to know is, "What can I do to help?" We recommend that you show the following section of this book to them so they'll know more about your problem and what they can reasonably do to help.

Suggestions for family and friends

1. *You can make a difference.* The people who help us the most are the people we are closest to. Your acceptance and support can be an important resource for someone you care about.

2. *Educate yourself about anxiety programs and their treatment.* Read about the problem so you are familiar with the difficulties and challenges your loved one faces. Keep in mind that people suffering from anxiety, panic, and phobias are in real distress. Fear, whether based on rational evidence or not, is very frightening and painful and can be extremely disabling. People cannot just "snap out of it," no matter how hard they try, without appropriate treatment. Offer to accompany your family member or friend to their therapist's office to learn about the disorder and the recommended treatment. Understand that your offer may be accepted or rejected. Remember that research shows these problems are treatable and people do get better.

3. *Be positive.* Anxiety sufferers can be perfectionists and hard on themselves. A positive and encouraging attitude will help them maintain a balanced perspective. At the same time, listening to and appreciating their struggles, and resisting the understandable urge to give unsolicited advice can be the most positive support you can offer.

4. *Be available.* Work with your family member or friend on the problem, if asked, including accompanying him or her on practice sessions. Find out, specifically, how you can be helpful to him or her before, during, and after practice.

5. *Allow your loved one to be in charge of his or her recovery.* The ability to make decisions and take independent action builds self-confidence and trust. Follow his or her lead in determining how, where, and when to work on the problem.

6. *Be patient.* Real progress can be gradual, and some ups and downs are part of the recovery process. Having a realistic time frame can reduce frustration. Get counseling or ask for support for yourself if you feel discouraged.

7. *Encourage your loved one's attempt at self help and independence.* Kindness, or a desire to protect others, may tempt you to do something for someone when they need to try it on

their own. This can lead to an unwanted result—depriving them of an opportunity to face fear and conquer it. Talk to your loved one about ways that you may, without meaning to, be making it harder for him or her to feel competent.

8. *Prepare for setbacks.* Setbacks are an unavoidable part of growth. Be ready to offer support when your loved one feels discouraged. Offer yourself the same support when the normal ups and downs of recovery frustrate you. Both of you need to keep in mind previous accomplishments. Both of you need praise and reassurance during this continuing effort. Reread the chapter "Why Am I Having Panic Attacks Again?" with the person you care about. Remember, you can't have a setback unless you've made some progress.

~ ~ ~

You already know about the tough times for yourself and for the person you care about. Jane's story will give you hope that better days lie ahead. Jane's husband couldn't fix things for her, but he encouraged her efforts, and now they both enjoy her recovery.

Jane's story

A strange thing happened to me on a short, one-hour plane trip. As the plane rumbled down the taxiway, my neck stiffened up, my heart started to race, and my mouth felt like cotton. Then my head felt heavy, but I also felt dizzy. The pilot announced we were all clear for takeoff and powered down on the throttle. I couldn't swallow, I couldn't breathe, I couldn't think. As the 727 lifted off the runway, I couldn't even make out the words my husband was saying to me. My brain froze, and my body belonged to somebody else.

Then, in less than sixty seconds, the plane was climbing steadily, and I felt a wave of relaxation sweep over me. I took a deep breath, shuddered, and I was fine again. Later, I realized that this episode had been a textbook panic attack. For the next sixteen years, my panic experience developed into a full-blown phobia about flying. I did fly from time to time, but I continued to have major panic attacks, so bad that for days ahead, I was nearly nonfunctional and incoherent.

Over the years, I fine-tuned my panic, focusing it on a sixty-second period from the time the airplane's tires lift off the ground to when the plane begins to level off to a more gradual climb. I could joke about it, but I was terrified of those sixty seconds. I tried everything to relax . . . I took Valium, I drank Scotch, I read trashy sex stories . . . I tried every diversion I could think of, but when those tires lifted off, I went into the ozone layer! My husband was wonderful, but he couldn't give me the magic words to stop the way I was feeling. What was I afraid of? After the first panic attack, I guess I was afraid that the same feeling would happen again, and I began to anticipate it.

When the episodes continued to occur, I developed a behavior pattern that I didn't know how to change, and it locked in.

The last straw came when I won a ten-day, all expenses paid trip to Europe and passed it up because I couldn't fly. I finally decided to get therapy and lick this thing once and for all. "Do you worry about other things besides flying?" was the first question the therapist asked. Ha! I could write a book on worry and anxiety. During the next few weeks, I discovered that my habit of worry was another learned behavior, and the anxiety I constantly experienced was the result of a steady flow of adrenaline, triggered by all that unnecessary worry.

I had learned from my parents to worry about things I couldn't control. My father had worried about going broke and ending up in the poorhouse and talked about this constantly. He also worried about aging and becoming helpless. Since I was a baby boomer, the threat of nuclear war was another ever-present danger.

My parents were not warm and loving, but they rewarded me for excellence. So, I became an overachiever, afraid of disappointing my parents and teachers, and later, my employers, friends, and spouse. Achieving became my way of being recognized and validated. In therapy, I confronted questions such as: Did I willingly promote my fear of flying as a means to get sympathy and attention? Did I cling to it as a way of being a special person? Was I afraid of being healthy and just like everyone else? It became clear that before I could learn any new behaviors about flying, I had to take a difficult first step and begin to prove to myself that I was an okay person on my own merits. I had to learn to trust myself and my emotions and reactions, and acknowledge that it was okay to say, "No, I don't want to do that," or "Gee, I don't know the answer."

The first time I flew successfully, I was ecstatic. I closed my eyes, took gentle, deep breaths, and gave in to the easy motion. When I opened my eyes, I was high in the sky. I have the tools at my command now, but I don't want to ever slip backwards, so I practice my newly learned relaxation techniques, imagining myself on a plane, eyes closed, and breathing steadily, deeply. These and other relaxing exercises have helped with everyday stresses and insomnia.

I have learned to fly again, literally as well as figuratively. And, as a bonus, I've stopped worrying about nuclear bombs and the poorhouse.

Appendix

*More information and materials
to support your recovery*

Medication management
of anxiety disorders

Many advances are being made in the development and use of medications to treat anxiety disorders. Since there are a number of options to consider, we recommend that you consult with a physician who specializes in this field. Your therapist can assist you with this issue.

The medication, dosage, and treatment schedule will vary from individual to individual, and it may also vary for you at different times during your recovery. If medication is prescribed, it will most likely be from one of the following categories of compounds:

- serotonin specific reuptake inhibitors (Prozac, Taxol, Zoloft, etc.)
- tricyclic antidepressants (Tofranil, Pamelor, etc.)
- MAO inhibitors (Nardil, Parnate, etc.)
- benzodiazepines (Xanax, Klonapin, etc.)
- buspirone (Buspar)
- beta blockers (Inderol, Tenormin)

Your physician will explain to you the medication of choice for your particular symptoms. We encourage you to communicate openly with your physician, asking questions so that you thoroughly understand your treatment.

How to find professional help

If you reside in the Greater San Diego or Boston areas, the authors of this book are available as resources for information and referral.

In the San Diego area, contact:
Shirley Babior, LCSW, MFCC
Director, Center for Anxiety and Stress Treatment
4225 Executive Square, Suite 1110
LaJolla, CA 92037
619-458-1066
e-mail address: health@stressrelease.com
Web site: www.stressrelease.com

In the Greater Boston area, contact:
Carol Goldman, LICSW
29 Commonwealth Avenue, Suite 809
Boston, MA 02116
617-236-1232

In other parts of the country, you may want to contact the Anxiety Disorders Association of America. It publishes a *National Treatment Directory*, which lists treatment programs throughout the nation. For more information write or call:

Anxiety Disorders Association of America
6000 Executive Blvd., Suite 200
Rockville, MD 20852
301-231-9350

If the directory lists no therapists in your area, ask local professional societies for names of psychologists, social workers, and psychiatrists who specialize in the treatment of anxiety disorders. If there is a college or university nearby, the various clinical departments make appropriate referrals. You can also help educate local therapists by sharing this book with them.

How to evaluate
a therapeutic program

When you locate a potential therapist, answers to the following questions will provide useful information that will help you decide whether the therapist's approach and program are appropriate for you. An initial assessment/consultation session will probably be needed in order to tailor the treatment program to your specific anxiety problems.

Questions

1. What is the therapist's basic approach to treatment? Does it involve exposing the client to anxiety-producing situations and sensations? What type of exposure methods are used?

2. What additional kinds of treatment are offered?

3. What is the average length of treatment? Are there provisions for follow-up after the initial therapy sessions?

4. How experienced is the therapist in treating anxiety disorders, and what is the therapist's training in this area?

5. In the program offered by this therapist, how is success defined?

6. How much does the treatment cost? Will your health insurance cover any of it?

How therapists
can use this book

Overcoming Panic, Anxiety, & Phobias can be a useful adjunct to psychotherapy or pharmacotherapy. If you are interested in familiarizing yourself with the professional literature on which these strategies are based, a bibliography is available from the authors on written request.

For all anxiety disorders, a thorough medical examination should be required prior to beginning treatment. Physical disorders may be present. We believe that a physician should always be consulted regarding the appropriateness of exposure treatment and the speed with which it can be carried out.

This book will help your clients with anxiety disorders to take an active role in their treatment. Ask your clients to fill out all of the worksheets in this book. This information will be a great help to both you and your client during all phases of treatment.

In our companion manual, *Working with Groups to Overcome Panic, Anxiety, & Phobias,* written specifically for therapists, we have highlighted the pages from this book that support the therapeutic goals of each session. Your clients may find that reading this material will provide the encouragement and motivation they need to keep them working productively on their problems between sessions.

You will find a description of this manual on page 129.

How support groups
can use this book

If you are in a support group, it is important that you focus on strategies for change. This book suggests a variety of coping strategies that will help your group support each member's journey toward recovery, and it explains their relevance to anxiety and phobias.

Your group may choose to practice relaxation together. You may record for one another the scripts from this book, or you may wish to purchase the relaxation tape described on the following page.

There are many ideas in this book that you might discuss as a group. Ask members to read a specific chapter prior to your meeting, then focus your discussion on that topic. You may want to invite professionals to share their insights.

Embarking on a program of recovery together can be easier than attempting it alone. Treat your group as a "mutual aid society." Remember that members can help one another no matter what specific anxiety symptoms each experiences.

For more help with planning your group's sessions, consult our book, *Working with Groups to Overcome Panic, Anxiety, & Phobias,* which is described on the following page.

Other resources

Working with Groups to Overcome Panic, Anxiety, & Phobias
Shirley Babior and Carol Goldman, softcover, $24.95

Written especially for therapists, this manual presents state of the art, well-researched treatment strategies for a variety of anxiety disorders. It includes treatment goals, basic anxiety-recovery exercises, and recovery enhancers that encourage lifestyle changes. The sessions in the therapist's manual are directly related to the chapters in *Overcoming Panic, Anxiety, & Phobias,* so material presented during therapy sessions can be reinforced by clients' reading and practice at home.

The book includes:
• Lecture guides
• Clinical case histories
• Worksheets and handouts
• An extensive bibliography

The material can be adapted for:
• Individual therapy
• Group therapy
• Worksite lectures
• All-day seminars or workshops

This book will serve as a valuable resource for providing and documenting appropriate, brief treatment for clients served by managed care companies.

Support groups will also find this manual useful. Sessions that require the leadership of a mental health professional are clearly marked. Other sessions can be used by nonprofessionals.

Calm Down, audiotape, $11.95
Breathe away stress and experience total body relaxation with the relaxation techniques from *Overcoming Panic, Anxiety, & Phobias.* Scripts adapted from this book and our book for therapists have been recorded against soothing background music.

For more information or to order, call 800-247-6789.

References

American Psychiatric Association Diagnostic and Statistical Manual of Mental Disorders, 4th Edition (1994). Washington, D.C.: American Psychiatric Association.

Barlow, D.H. (1988). *Anxiety and Its Disorders: The Nature and Treatment of Anxiety and Panic.* New York: Guilford Press.

Barlow, D.H. (1993). *Clinical Handbook of Psychological Disorders* (2nd ed.) (ch.1, p. 1–47); (ch.3, p.99–136); (ch.4, p.137–188). New York: Guilford Press.

Beck, A.T., G. Emery, and R. Greenberg (1985). *Anxiety Disorders and Phobia: A Cognitive Perspective.* New York: Guilford Press.

Burns, S.D. (1980). *Feeling Good: The New Mood Therapy.* New York: William Morrow & Company.

Ost, L.G. (1988). "Applied relaxation, description of a coping technique, and review of controlled studies." *Behavior Research and Therapy* (25, p. 397–410).

Taylor, C.B., and B. Arnow (1988). *The Nature and Treatment of Anxiety Disorders.* New York: International Universities Press.

Young, J.E. (1990). *Cognitive Therapy for Personality Disorders: A Schema-Focused Approach.* Sarasota, Fla.: Professional Resource Exchange, Inc.

About the authors

Shirley Babior, LCSW, MFCC, is a therapist in private practice in San Diego, California, where she is Director of the Center for Anxiety and Stress Treatment. She specializes in treating anxiety disorders, in groups and individually. As a Certified Employee Assistance Professional, Shirley provides services to employees suffering from anxiety and stress in the workplace. She has lectured on the treatment of anxiety disorders at numerous professional meetings and adult education workshops. Shirley is a former regional governor of the Phobia Society of America and board member of the Society of Behavioral Medicine.

Carol Goldman, LICSW, was director of Behavior Associates from 1977 to 1989. She is a founding director of the Boston Institute of Cognitive-Behavior Therapies, a training program for mental health professionals. As the past president of the Greater Boston Phobia Society, Carol worked with professionals and anxiety sufferers to increase public awareness about anxiety disorders. Carol is currently in private practice in Boston, Massachusetts. She specializes in cognitive-behavior therapy, family systems, and couples therapy, and provides training to professionals on brief treatment and managed care.

Worksheets

On the following pages, you will find duplicates of all the worksheets that are printed in this book. We have reprinted them here so that you can photocopy them conveniently. Because many of the worksheets should be used repeatedly, we encourage you to make several blank copies prior to completing them.

Either photocopy the pages directly from the book, or, if you find it to be more convenient, clip them out first.

Anxiety and Panic Responses
Targets for Change

Part I: Anxiety producing episode

Date _____ Time_____

What brought on your feelings of anxiety or panic?

_____

_____

Circle your anxiety level:

  0   1   2   3   4   5   6   7   8   9   10
  none   mild   moderate   strong

Part II: Anxiety and panic responses

a. Physical sensations

List the physical sensations you felt during your anxiety response, e.g., dizziness, shortness of breath, blushing, sweating, muscle tension. Circle the three that frighten you most.

_____

_____

_____

b. Thoughts and images

List the thoughts you had when anticipating or experiencing your anxiety response, e.g., "I'm having a heart attack," "I'm losing control," or "Something terrible will happen."

_____

_____

_____

c. Behaviors and actions

List the behaviors you exhibited or actions you took as a result of your anxiety response. _____

_____

The Costs of Anxiety

Anxiety has hurt my relationships with _____

_____

_____

Anxiety has limited my life by _____

_____

_____

Life Without Severe Anxiety

When I am free of severe anxiety, I will feel_____

_____

_____

I will be free to do _____

_____

_____

My Worry Cycle

My thoughts or images are _____

_____

_____

_____

My physical sensations are_____

_____

_____

My actions are _____

_____

_____

My Panic Cycle

My panic attacks are triggered by _____

_____

My physical sensations are _____

_____

_____

My thoughts and images are _____

_____

My actions are _____

_____

Other activities and places that I now fear include _____

_____

Catching Anxious Thoughts

The last time I felt panicky, I thought _____

_____

_____

Take this book or some notepaper with you and catch the anxious thoughts right after they occur. What are the most important anxious messages you are telling yourself?

_____

_____

_____

Anxiety Rating Scale

Many people can't discriminate between different levels of anxiety or panic. They feel either calm or anxious. To help you become aware of your own intermediate levels of anxiety, complete this worksheet form, being as specific as you can.

As you experiment with the coping strategies you will be learning, refer to this worksheet in order to discover what strategies work best for you at different levels of anxiety.

Level 10: extreme anxiety

When my anxiety is at level 10, my thoughts are_____

_____

_____

My bodily sensations are _____

_____

_____

My behaviors include _____

_____

Level 8: on the verge of extreme anxiety

When my anxiety is at level 8, my thoughts are_____

_____

_____

My bodily sensations are _____

_____

_____

My behaviors include _____

_____

_____

Level 6: severe anxiety

When my anxiety is at level 6, my thoughts are _____

_____

_____

My bodily sensations are _____

_____

_____

My behaviors include _____

_____

Level 4: moderate anxiety

When my anxiety is at level 4, my thoughts are _____

_____

_____

My bodily sensations are _____

_____

_____

My behaviors include _____

_____

Level 2: mild anxiety

When my anxiety is at level 2, my thoughts are _____

_____

_____

My bodily sensations are _____

_____

_____

My behaviors include _____

_____

My Goals

List two to four goals you'd like to achieve in the next one to three months. Fill in the action strategies as you learn new coping skills.

Goal 1 _____

Action strategies to achieve my goal:

    a. _____

    b. _____

    c. _____

    d. _____

Goal 2 _____

Action strategies to achieve my goal:

    a. _____

    b. _____

    c. _____

    d. _____

Goal 3 _____

Action strategies to achieve my goal:

    a. _____

    b. _____

    c. _____

    d. _____

Goal 4 _____

Action strategies to achieve my goal:

    a. _____

    b. _____

    c. _____

    d. _____

Tension/Relaxation Rating

Rate your feelings before and after the relaxation exercise from 0 (most relaxed) to 10 (most tense).

Date	Before the exercise	After the exercise	List the events, thoughts, and physical sensations that had contributed to your feelings of stress.

Getting to the Heart of the Matter

My peril prediction _____

_____

_____

If that occurs, what might happen next?	What would be so bad about that?
If that occurs, what might happen next?	What would be so bad about that?
If that occurs, what might happen next?	What would be so bad about that?
If that occurs, what might happen next?	What would be so bad about that?

Looking at the Odds: Strengthening the Rational You

a. Day/time:

b. Anxiety cue (events/thoughts/sensations):

c. My peril prediction:

d. Odds that my peril prediction will occur (0–100%):

e. Evidence for the likelihood of my peril prediction occuring:

f. Evidence against the likelihood of my peril prediction occuring:

g. New odds that my peril prediction will occur (0-100%):

h. New self-talk after reviewing all the evidence:

Looking at the Danger: Strengthening the Rational You

a. Day/time:

b. Anxiety cue (events/thoughts/sensations):

c. My peril prediction:

d. Danger severity rating (0–100%):

e. Evidence for catastrophe if my peril prediction happens:

f. Evidence against catastrophe if my peril prediction happens:

g. New danger severity rating (0-100%):

h. New self-talk after reviewing all the evidence:

Security Moves			
Security move	Challenge strategy	What happened	Benefits for the future

Exposure List

List situations, thoughts or images, and physical sensations you are anxious or worried about, or which may cause panic, then write a number from 0 to 10 that represents the intensity of your feelings.

Situations, thoughts, and physical sensations	Anxiety or panic rating

Exposure in Imagination

My peril prediction _____

_____

_____

If that occurs, what might happen next?	What would be so bad about that?
If that occurs, what might happen next?	What would be so bad about that?
If that occurs, what might happen next?	What would be so bad about that?
If that occurs, what might happen next?	What would be so bad about that?

Sensory Exercise (after medical clearance)

Add to the list of exercises below any others that trigger physical sensations similar to those that you fear. On a scale from 1 to 10, rate each sensation's intensity, then the intensity of the anxiety it provokes. On the next line, describe how this sensation relates to what you feel during anxiety.

Intensity of
Sensation / Anxiety

1. Hyperventilate (30 sec.)   ____   ____

_____

2. Spin in a chair (1 min.)   ____   ____

_____

3. Hold your breath (30 sec.)   ____   ____

_____

4. Shake your head from side to side (30 sec.)   ____   ____

_____

5. Run in place (30 sec.)   ____   ____

_____

6. Bend quickly, then straighten up (30 sec.)   ____   ____

_____

7. Rapidly run up and down stairs (30 sec.)   ____   ____

_____

8. Put head between legs, then raise it (30 sec.) ____   ____

_____

        ____   ____

_____

        ____   ____

_____

Exposure Strategy List

1. Anxiety sensations are normal physical reactions and not harmful.

2. Worry is not a predictor of outcome.

3. Focus on the Rational You. Don't allow the Frightened You to take over.

4. Tell yourself, "I can enter my exposure session without my security moves and be safe."

5. Practice your slow, gentle breathing.

6. Some anxiety is normal and to be expected.

7. Progress is gradual—recovery takes time. Be patient with yourself.

8. Focus on what is really happening to you and around you—not what you fear might happen.

9. Wait for your fear to decrease and notice when it begins to fade. If you leave an exposure session, return as soon as possible to continue practice.

10. Each practice situation is an opportunity to test your peril predictions.

11. Celebrate your successes, no matter how small. They will add up.